LEARN TO COOK

it's easy when you know how

LOW GI

70 STEP-BY-STEP RECIPES • LORNA RHODES

INDEX

To my trusted tester Robin, who has benefited from Low GI to lose weight, and
to Dan and Jenny, who have inspired me to write recipes for a young couple.

This edition published 2007 for Index Books Ltd

HarperThorsons
An Imprint of HarperCollins*Publishers*
77–85 Fulham Palace Road
Hammersmith, London W6 8JB

The website address is: www.thorsonselement.com

and *HarperThorsons* are trademarks of
HarperCollins*Publishers* Limited

Published by HarperThorsons 2005

1 3 5 7 9 10 8 6 4 2

© Lorna Rhodes 2005

Lorna Rhodes asserts the moral right to
be identified as the author of this work

Photography by Sue Jorgensen
Food for photography prepared by Lorna Rhodes,
assisted by Juliana Bastos Delgado

A catalogue record for this book
is available from the British Library

ISBN-13: 9780007788583
ISBN-10: 0007788584

Printed and bound in Hong Kong by
Printing Express

contents

introduction

Cooking and eating delicious food should be fun and not a chore. We are overwhelmed with a huge choice and abundance of food these days, yet I hear people say they haven't time or haven't the confidence to cook. Here is a book to help you understand how to cook and how to eat in an enjoyable, healthy way without complicated rules.

The recipes in this book have been created with modern cooks in mind: people with busy lives who insist, nevertheless, on eating the best, freshest and healthiest foods they can. The recipes can be scaled up – or down – to suit your needs. Flexibility is built in: you can take leftovers to work next day, or use the soups and salads as starters, or add extra ingredients for a weekend lunch at home. Throughout the book, tips and full explanations are included to help you make the most of all the ingredients to suit your lifestyle.

WHAT IS LOW GI?

The Glycaemic Index, or GI, measures how quickly carbohydrate foods affect the blood glucose (blood sugar levels). Carbohydrates with a high GI convert more quickly to glucose than those with a low GI rating. A simple rule to remember is that foods that take longer to digest have a lower GI than foods which are processed such as bread made with white flour.

Choosing the right type of carbohydrates (fruits, vegetables and wholegrain cereals), combined with lean sources of protein and unsaturated fats, is the key to healthy eating. This balance provides us with a constant source of energy. Many people following a low-GI diet have found that their energy levels improve, they have a fuller feeling for longer and are eating more healthily. The other plus is it can help you control your weight more easily, and if you watch the portion sizes, you will lose weight, too.

But this is not a diet book. Who wants to count calories, fats or points for each meal?

Without even having to think about it, by following these recipes you will be eating plenty of fresh fruits and vegetables that will provide lots of super nutrients, particularly antioxidants which help to boost the immune system, while enjoying a variety of tastes and textures in your meals.

As for ingredients, try to buy the best you can afford, and remember: The most memorable meals are often the simplest.

What Makes a Healthy Low-GI Diet?

It is important to understand which carbohydrate foods have a low GI and give a slow rise in glucose in your bloodstream. Generally, the less processed the carbohydrate, the lower the GI.

STARCHES

- **Bread** – In many supermarkets, low-GI breads (such as wholemeal pitta bread) carry a low-GI symbol, but granary, wholegrain or wholemeal breads made with stoneground flour are also good, as are rye and soya breads.
- **Cereals** – Most of us will eat cereal for breakfast, and it's a good way to kick-start the day with an intake of carbohydrate, and prevent mid-morning hunger pangs. Choose cereals with the least amount of processing and additives, particularly sugar. Oats are perfect, so learn to love porridge or scatter some oats over fresh fruit for breakfast.
- **Grains** – Wholegrains that have not been highly processed are best. Look for buckwheat, barley, bulgur wheat, millet and quinoa. Couscous is medium GI but still a good choice as an occasional change of pace. Barley flakes can be included in home-made muesli, and try pearl barley in soups and stews. Choose Basmati, wild, or brown rice rather than short-grain varieties or the refined long-grain rice.
- **Potatoes** – The best choice is boiled small new potatoes. Avoid chips, jacket potatoes or mashed potatoes. (Interestingly, mashing potatoes breaks down the carbohydrate and so raises the GI.)

  To balance the high GI of a baked potato, you can serve it with baked beans which will reduce the impact of the potato to make it a medium-GI meal.
- **Pasta** – Most pastas are low GI because the flour used (durum) contains protein. Do not eat large amounts, though, and cook only to al dente, as the softer it is the higher the GI. Noodles can be eaten in moderate amounts, but try to use glass or cellophane noodles.

FRUITS AND VEGETABLES

Fruits and vegetables are essential for a healthy diet as they provide essential vitamins and minerals that boost the immune system. It is recommended that we eat five portions a day; this should not be difficult if you include fruit as between-meal snacks, and include lots of vegetables in your main dishes. Here are some interesting facts about fruits, vegetables and GI:

- Always eat fruits and vegetables in their whole form rather than as juice. Juice is processed and therefore is digested more quickly.
- The more acidic the fruit, the lower its GI. Adding lime or lemon juice to a dish lowers its overall GI content.
- If using canned fruit, look for fruit in natural juice rather than syrup, which has a higher GI.
- The more fructose a fruit contains, the lower its GI as fructose is hard to digest. You can now buy fruit sugar, which has lower GI than cane sugar and it is used in most of the baking recipes in this book.
- Vegetables should be the main focus of your meals. Try to eat salads as often as possible. The high-fibre content helps to slow down digestion and lower the GI of other foods. Some exceptions are parsnips, swedes/turnips and beetroot, and sweet vegetables such as pumpkin, so eat these in moderation.

PROTEIN FOODS

Protein foods are essential for tissue repair in the body, for muscle tone and growth, healthy skin and nails, and in the manufacture of hormones.

Protein in the diet slows down the digestive process, which is important in controlling blood-sugar levels and keeping you feeling satisfied and full. Too much protein can make the body acidic, which can cause all sorts of imbalances, whereas a diet high in vegetable helps to keep an alkaline balance, which is preferable.

About 15–20% of your daily diet should be protein foods. The best sources are lean meats trimmed of any visible fats, skinless poultry, unbuttered or uncrumbed fish and seafood, low-fat dairy foods, eggs, beans or soya-based products such as tofu.

Vegetable-based proteins such as lentils, beans, soya beans, soya bean curd, peas, corn and nuts (such as Brazil nuts, almonds, pecans and walnuts) are known to lower cholesterol levels and help to balance hormones, so we should all be eating more of them. They are inexpensive and versatile in dishes; many of the recipes in this book explore their use.

FATS

Fats are absolutely essential in your diet and for your digestion. While low-fat foods are beneficial for weight loss, it is important to know which fats are good for us and which are not. The good fats are mostly vegetable-based and found in oils such as sunflower and corn oils. The best oils are those high in monounsaturated fats such as rapeseed (canola) and olive oil. These are the oils used in most of the recipes in this book. The essential fatty acids (EFAs) found in these oils are necessary for every cell in the body. Additional good sources are seeds such as sesame, linseed and pumpkin, and avocados and oily fish. In addition, oily fish contain Omega 3, which is vitally important for brain function and helps protect the heart.

Fats to avoid are called saturated fats. These tend to come from animal sources; they are solid at room temperature and include butter, cheese and fatty meats.

Many processed foods such as cakes, pies, sausages, margarines and burgers contain hydrogenated or 'trans' fats, which should be avoided as much as possible as they can clog the arteries and cause heart disease.

Note that it is the combination of protein and fats that gives nuts and seeds their low GI. Spreads made from nuts and seeds will also have a low GI.

WATER

Water is very important to health. Ideally we should drink 8 glasses of water a day. You will also ingest water naturally when you eat plenty of fruits.

Getting the Balance Right

- High GI + low GI = medium GI. But try not to eat more than one high-GI food or two medium-GI foods in one day.
- Try to add something acidic to your meal or dish, for example lemon or lime juice slows down the conversion of carbs to glucose. Vinegar in a salad dressing has the same effect.
- If you eat a high-GI food, try to keep the portion size small.

QUICK TIPS

- Eat three meals a day. Never skip breakfast. Make sure your breakfast contains low GI carbohydrates and low-fat protein.
- Eat three snacks a day such as fruit, seeds and nuts, oatcakes, plain or low-fat yogurt or fromage frais, slice of fruit loaf, 2 squares 70% cocoa chocolate.
- Try to incorporate as great a variety of low-GI ingredients in your meals to make them interesting and provide a wide range of nutrients.
- Limit your intake of coffee or tea to 2 cups a day. Cut out sugary energy drinks and fizzy drinks. Get into the habit of drinking more water.

Making the Right Choices

SHOPPING

Buying the right ingredients will give you the best chance of eating a healthy low-GI diet. Keep a well-stocked larder of non-perishable foods so there is always something on hand if you have no time to shop. Whilst recognizing that supermarkets are a convenient way to shop, look out for farmer's market and try to buy local produce when you can. If it suits your lifestyle, consider having a box of organic vegetables and fruits delivered to your home, a sure way of having a plentiful supply.

Low-GI Supplies

- Stone ground plain wholemeal flour, buckwheat flour
- Fruit sugar
- Cans of pulses, preferably no-sugar added, reduced-sugar baked beans, dried beans, lentils, pearl barley
- Pasta
- Canned tomatoes, tomato purée
- Canned tuna, salmon, sardines, crabmeat
- Oats, preferable traditional, sugar-free muesli, oat bran, All bran
- Pumpernickel, high-fibre crispbread
- Seeds and nuts
- Low-salt vegetable stock powder
- Curry pastes
- Dried fruits, e.g. apricots, raisins and sultanas/golden raisins
- Dried herbs and spices, mustard, vinegars, Worcester-shire sauce
- Sunflower, rapeseed/canola, olive oil, vegetable oil sprays
- Canned fruit in juice
- Herb and fruit teas

Medium-GI Supplies

- Bulgur wheat, couscous, Basmati Rice, brown and wild rice
- Tortilla wraps
- Shredded wheat, Weetabix
- Corn oil, peanut butter, sesame oil, vegetable oil

Low-GI Fresh Ingredients

- Semi-skimmed milk (but use skimmed if trying to lose weight), unsweetened soy, almond or rice milk
- Low-fat plain yogurt, low-fat or fat free fromage frais. Fruit yogurt (no fat or sugar)
- Low-fat or fat-free cottage cheese
- Extra lean beef, lean back bacon, skinless chicken breast, turkey breast or leg, veal, lean ham, rabbit, seafood

- Apples, berries, cherries, clementines, mandarins/tangerines, grapefruit, grapes, kiwi, lemons, limes, peaches and nectarines, oranges, pears, plums, rhubarb
- Unsweetened apple, cranberry, grapefruit, orange juice
- Avocados, asparagus, aubergine/eggplant, beans (runner and green), beansprouts, broccoli, Brussels sprouts, cabbage, carrots, cauliflower, celery, courgettes/zucchini, cucumber, leeks, onions, lettuce, mushrooms, olives, peas, peppers, spinach, tomatoes, fresh ginger and garlic

Medium-GI Fresh Ingredients

- Eggs, soft margarine (non-hydrogenated), fruit yogurt, reduced or half-fat cheese, reduced-fat crème fraiche, low-fat ice-cream, light cream cheese
- Lean lamb, lean pork, sirloin steak, lean minced beef
- Apricots, bananas, cantaloupe melon, honeydew melon, mangoes, dried fruit, papaya, pineapple, raisins and sultanas/golden raisins
- Artichokes, beetroot, corn, potatoes (boiled new), sweet potatoes

Cooking Equipment

Most of us will have some basic equipment in our kitchens – bowls of various sizes, wooden spoons, cutlery, can opener and corkscrew. Where special equipment is needed in a recipe, you will find a reminder at the beginning, but here are some recommendations to make cooking easier and maybe save some time:

- Kitchen scales – very useful if baking, when accuracy is needed
- A really good-quality, large, heavy non-stick frying pan – even better, a small one, too
- A wok, but failing that you can make stir-fries in the frying pan
- A griddle pan, preferably cast iron
- Saucepan with steamer: steaming vegetables is a good way of cooking to retain colour, flavour and the nutrients, especially in green leafy vegetables
- A strong, heavy roasting tin for cooking vegetables in the oven
- Small non-stick saucepan
- A casserole dish with a tight-fitting lid. If flameproof it will save a lot of bother when cooking stews and casseroles
- Good-quality baking sheet
- Chopping boards: try to have different ones, particularly for raw meats, vegetables and fruits (nothing worse than tasting garlic on some chopped pineapple)
- Measuring spoons – essential if you are not sure about how much of certain herbs and spices you need to add to a dish
- A grater with different grades for fine and coarse shredding. Modern planers are fabulous for grating the rind from citrus fruits
- Fish slice or spatula for lifting and turning food. Tongs are also useful to turn pieces of chicken or meat over
- Rubber spatulas make mixing food and for scraping out bowls easy
- Colander or large sieve
- A timer, unless you can keep a close eye on the clock without distractions while cooking

- Lemon squeezer, pastry cutters, pastry brush, vegetable peeler, scissors, rolling pin, oven gloves, cling film/plastic wrap and foil
- And, it goes without saying, a set of good-quality knives

If your budget allows:
- A hand-held blender for blitzing soups or even making smoothies
- Food processor, with shredding and slicing blades – will save you time chopping and slicing
- Hand-held electric mixer, great for whisking egg white
- A muffin pan
- A sauté pan with lid
- Pestle and mortar for grinding up whole spices
- A selection of baking tins and a loaf tin for making cakes

A Note on Cooking Temperatures

How do you bring something to the boil, and what does 'simmer' mean?

I have seen people put a pan on the stove, turn the heat on and leave it to boil away and burn the food – STOP! Some foods need gentler cooking and some attention.

To bring any liquid to the boil, turn the heat up to maximum until bubbles break the surface of the liquid. The only time you will need to cook at full boil is when you want to reduce a liquid's volume. For anything else, such as cooking pasta and rice, you should reduce the heat once boiling point is reached. 'Simmer' means heating at just below boiling point, so turn the heat down so that the surface of the liquid trembles with small

bubbles. For any mixture of ingredients that need to be simmered for more than 5 minutes, you will need to keep stirring them from time to time to keep them from sticking to the bottom of the pan.

Notes on the Recipes

- Most cookbooks assume that you have some knowledge and cooking skills. Not everyone does, however, so this book includes step-by-step explanations on how to prepare certain ingredients. There are also tips on what to watch out for so you will gain in confidence in the kitchen and enjoy your efforts at preparing tasty, healthy meals.
- Always assemble your ingredients and equipment before you start. The recipes in this book have been written so you use your time wisely in the kitchen; if at any stage you are distracted while preparing part of a recipe, remove any food already cooking from the hob while you catch up.
- Ingredients are given in metric and, where applicable, cup measurements. Use only one set of measurements.
- When measuring dry ingredients such as spices and baking powder, they should be level. Chopped herbs are given as 'rounded' (when they are slightly domed on the spoon) or 'heaped' (when the ingredients are piled onto the spoon).

I wish you happy cooking and many memorable meals ahead!

20 Kitchen Rules

1. Always wash your hands before preparing food and dry them on some paper towel, not a tea towel.
2. Always wash and dry fresh produce before use.
3. Wear an apron to protect your clothes from splashes.
4. Keep your work surfaces clean – use an anti-bacterial cleaner on all work surfaces and chopping boards.
5. Do not lick your fingers and don't keep tasting and stirring with the same spoon, despite what you may see chefs doing on TV!
6. Wash tea towels regularly and replace the washing-up brush and scourers before they start looking too yucky.
7. Check sell-by and use-by dates before buying food.
8. Foods should be refrigerated as soon as possible after purchase. Any stored food that starts to grow mould, or smells off, should be thrown away. Do not refreeze frozen food once it has thawed.
9. Keep food stored in the fridge covered or wrapped, to avoid it drying out and avoid cross-contamination. Do not store raw and cooked meat on the same shelf in the refrigerator. Put raw meat on the bottom shelf so that juices can't drip onto other foods.
10. Do not overfill the fridge or it will not maintain a low enough temperature.
11. All cooked food should be allowed to cool to room temperature before being put in the fridge.
12. Frozen meat should be thawed thoroughly before cooking.
13. Wipe spills from the floor immediately so you don't slip.
14. When re-heating food, always make sure it is piping hot and not just lukewarm.
15. Store the contents of half-used cans of food in china, glass or plastic containers. Never put an open can in the fridge, as the tin can corrode.
16. Don't leave pan handles sticking out from the stove while cooking, they could easily be knocked over.
17. Don't use metal or foil containers in the microwave.
18. Don't leave kitchen paper, tea towels or oven gloves near the hob/stove-top where they could catch fire while cooking.
19. Keep the sink clean and free from vegetable peelings and any other bits of food.
20. Some people suffer from food allergies. If you are entertaining guests, check if they suffer from allergies before you prepare food for them.

Kick-start the day with something fresh and tasty. Keep plenty of fresh fruit on hand to turn into a smoothie, chop into muesli or wholegrain cereal, or slice on top of toast spread with a low-fat cheese. And try to add some seeds to your breakfast such as linseed, hemp or sunflower, for extra goodness.

rise & shine

blueberry pancakes   **SERVES 4**

Blueberries are one of nature's superfoods, providing a high level of antioxidants. They can be expensive at certain times in the year, but for food value and taste, they're well worth it.

fresh blueberries	150g/1 cup
orange	1 medium
light brown sugar	1 tbs
cornflour	1 tsp
water	1 tbs

pancakes

all-purpose wholemeal flour	100g/¾ cup
baking powder	1 tsp
porridge oats	40g/½ cup
caster/superfine sugar	1 tbs
eggs	2 large
semi-skimmed milk	180ml/¾ cup
vanilla extract	1 tsp
butter, melted	25g/2tbs/¼ stick

equipment

Sieve	Whisk
Grater	Electric beater
Small saucepan	Large non-stick frying
1 small bowl	pan
1 medium bowl	Pastry brush
1 large bowl	Palette knife or
Measuring jug	spatula

- Put the blueberries in a sieve and rinse under cold water. Grate the zest from the orange into a small saucepan, squeeze the juice and add the sugar. Bring to the boil and boil for 1 minute, then add the blueberries, bring back to the boil and turn down the heat. In a medium bowl, blend the cornflour and water and add to the blueberry mixture. Stir over medium heat until the syrup thickens and the blueberries release some juice and begin to soften. Remove from the heat and set to one side.

- To make the batter, put the flour, baking powder, oats and sugar into a large bowl. Separate the eggs (cracking each one and letting the egg white fall into a medium bowl while retaining the yolk in the shell). Drop the yolks into the measuring jug with the milk and add the vanilla. Whisk.

- Pour this mixture into the dry ingredients and combine.

- With an electric beater, whisk the egg whites until stiff, then carefully fold into the batter.

- Heat the frying pan to medium-high, and lightly brush with melted butter. Drop 2 or 3 tablespoons of the batter into the pan, leaving space in between, as the pancakes will spread. Cook for about 2 minutes – bubbles will come to the surface. Take a look at the underside by lifting the edge of a pancake with a small palette knife or the edge of a fish slice. When golden, turn the pancake over and cook a further 2 minutes until golden.

- Repeat with the remaining batter, brushing the pan each time with melted butter, to make 8 pancakes.

- Serve topped with the blueberry sauce.

FROM START TO FINISH: 25 MINUTES

step-by-step

oranges

BUYING AND STORING

There are three main varieties of orange: the smooth-skinned Valencia, the thicker-skinned navel and the bitter Seville (which is used for making marmalade). Look for bright, firm fruit and avoid fruit if it feels puffy or the skin feels soft. Avoid wrinkled, darkened or damaged fruit.

Store in a cool place or in the refrigerator during hot weather. Do not stack oranges in a bowl as the ones underneath tend to become mouldy quickly; this also applies to the smaller citrus fruits: clementines, mandarins and satsumas.

HEALTHY BENEFITS

Oranges are a good source of vitamin C, but this vitamin content depletes as the fruit ages, so try to eat the freshest fruit possible. The high vitamin C in oranges is essential for maintaining healthy blood cells and increasing resistance to infections. Vitamin C is one of the best known anti-ageing antioxidants and it may even help to protect against asthma, bronchitis, cancers and gum disease. Oranges lower blood cholesterol, boost the immune system and improve iron absorption and the healing of wounds. Oranges provide sugars, some dietary fibre and very small amounts of protein, they also contain folic acid. They have an energy value of 35 kcals per 100g.

Eating oranges therefore helps to maintain energy levels and keeps skin and mucous membranes in good condition. For maximum nutritional benefit, eat the whole fruit rather than juice.

PREPARATION TECHNIQUES

Wash oranges thoroughly before use as they may have a wax coating to protect them from moisture loss.

The rind or zest can be grated at varying thicknesses depending on the grater used or one of the newer planers. For fine strips use a tool called a zester which has small holes to give very thin strips or rind. Alternatively pare off the rind with a vegetable peeler and cut into very thin strips. Whether grating or paring, avoid the white pith as it is bitter.

TO MAKE SEGMENTS:

1 Wash the orange thoroughly.

2 Slice a little of the peel and pith from the top and bottom of the orange so that you can just see the flesh.

3 Stand the fruit on a board and cut away all the skin and pith with a serrated knife.

4 Trim off any remaining pith.

5 Hold the fruit over a bowl to catch the juice and cut down the sides of the membranes to remove the segments.

6 Once the first segment is removed it is easier to cut out the remainder.

apricot & orange compote SERVES 4–6

Apricots are both high in fibre and high in antioxidants, helping the body to keep healthy by fighting free radicals, which can cause disease. They taste great too, and are perfect for snacking and for a breakfast fruit serving.

dried apricots	350g/1¾ cups
star anise	2
cloves	2
fruit sugar	2 tbs
oranges	3 medium
water	300ml/1⅓ cups

equipment

Medium saucepan   Citrus juicer

Citrus zester   Serrated knife

- Put the apricots into the saucepan, add the star anise, cloves and fruit sugar.
- Peel the rind from one of the oranges with a zester and add the orange rind strips to the pan, squeeze the juice and add it along with the water.
- Bring to the boil then reduce the heat, cover the pan and simmer for 15 minutes. Remove from the heat and leave to cool.
- Meanwhile, peel the 2 remaining oranges and then cut them into segments (see page 7). Add these to the apricots with any juices that escape while cutting the segments and squeeze the juice from the oranges' membranes into the apricot mixture before discarding.
- Cover and refrigerate overnight.

FROM START TO FINISH: 20 MINUTES, PLUS COOLING

cook's tip

A dollop of yogurt and a scattering of muesli makes this fruit salad extra good and good for you!

dreamland smoothies **SERVES 1–2**

For a fast and filling breakfast in a glass, packed with vitamins, these smoothies are an easy and delicious way to include lots of fruit in your diet and keep you going through the morning.

apple & blackberry smoothie

You can also use blackcurrants or blueberries as an alternative. If you prefer a sweeter smoothie add ½ tsp liquid honey.

dessert apple	1
blackberries	75g/½ cup
semi-skimmed milk	150ml/⅔ cup
low-fat natural yogurt	3 tbs

equipment

Vegetable peeler   Food processor or blender

- Peel and core the apple, cut into chunks and put into the food processor or blender with the washed blackberries, milk and yogurt.
- Blend until smooth.

FROM START TO FINISH: 5 MINUTES

mango & melon smoothie

If you cannot get fresh mangoes, use a large (400g/14-oz) can of peaches in natural juice, but drain the juice off first.

ripe mango	1 medium
cantaloupe melon	½
fresh orange juice	200ml/7fl oz
	(made from 3–4 oranges, depending on their size)

equipment

Sharp knife   Measuring jug
Food processor or blender   Citrus squeezer

- Peel the skin off the mango and cut the flesh away from the large stone. Roughly chop. Discard the seeds from the melon and scoop out the flesh into the food processor or blender, then add the orange juice.
- Blend until smooth.
- Enjoy!

FROM START TO FINISH: 10 MINUTES

fruity porridge **SERVES 1**

spice blend

ground cloves	⅛ tsp
ground allspice	⅛ tsp
ground cinnamon	½ tsp
demerara/light brown sugar	4 tsp

porridge

peach or nectarine	1 small
porridge oats	45g/½ cup
water	115ml/½ cup
semi-skimmed milk	115ml/½ cup
sugar or honey	to sweeten to taste

equipment

Glass jar   Small saucepan
Sharp knife

- Put all the spices and sugar into a jar and shake together.
- Slice the fruit, discarding the stone.
- Put the oats, water and milk into a saucepan. If you like, add a vanilla pod to infuse a sweet flavour in the mix. Heat and, when it comes to the boil, lower the heat and cook for 3–4 minutes, stirring all the time.
- If you prefer sloppier porridge, add a dash more milk. Pour into a bowl, add the fruit on top and sprinkle over some of the spice blend. Serve with a spoonful of plain yogurt.

FROM START TO FINISH: 5 MINUTES

overnight muesli **SERVES 1**

Experiment with other fruits such as a chopped peach or nectarine, or some fresh berries. Alternatively, add a few raisins to the oats before you leave them to soak overnight.

jumbo oats (preferably organic)	3 tbs
apple or pineapple juice (apple and elderflower juice is good)	4 tbs
apple or firm pear	1
lemon juice (optional)	1 tbs
plain yogurt	2 tbs
chopped nuts	1 tbs

equipment

2 bowls   Grater

- Last thing at night, put the oats into a bowl, pour over the juice then mix together and leave in the refrigerator overnight.
- Grate the apple or pear, add a squeeze of lemon juice if desired, then mix into the oats.
- You can either stir the yogurt and nuts into the muesli or spoon on top.

FROM START TO FINISH: 5 MINUTES' PREPARATION PLUS OVERNIGHT SOAKING

kiwi cottage cheese on rye **SERVES 1**

Other fresh fruit, such as peaches or nectarines, which does not need peeling, is also great for this recipe.

kiwi fruit	1 large
rye bread or seeded pumpernickel bread	1 thick slice (about 50g/2oz)
low-fat cottage cheese	1 heaped tbs (about 50g/2oz)
freshly ground black pepper	
sunflower or pumpkin seeds	2 tsp

equipment

Small sharp knife   Toaster

- Cut the ends off the kiwi fruit and then cut the skin off. Slice.
- Toast the bread then arrange the slices of fruit over. Spoon over the cottage cheese, season with black pepper then top with the seeds.

FROM START TO FINISH: 5 MINUTES

peanut butter & banana wraps **SERVES 1**

Slices of apple, pineapple, kiwi or mango would be equally delicious for these wraps.

wheat tortilla	1
crunchy peanut butter	1 heaped tbs (approx 30g)
banana	1 small or ½ large

equipment

Butter knife

- Warm the tortilla either in the microwave for a few seconds or under the grill/broiler.
- Spread the peanut butter over the middle of the tortilla.
- Thickly slice the banana and place on top. Fold one edge towards the centre, then fold the two sides over the filling to make a pocket.

FROM START TO FINISH: 5 MINUTES

We all love a little something between meals, and fruit is the perfect convenience snack. For extra treats, have fun with a baking session, so you have a supply of healthy goodies either for yourself or for when friends drop in.

healthy snacking

apple ginger cake bars   SERVES 12

This recipe calls for using a rubber spatula, which is more flexible than a metal spoon and helps you get to the mixture at the bottom of the bowl, so you can be sure the mixture at the bottom of the bowl is scraped up and mixed in properly.

soft sunflower margarine	115g/½ cup
fruit sugar	115g/½ cup
eggs	2 large
plain/all-purpose wholemeal flour	225g/1½ cups
baking powder	2 tsp
ground cinnamon	1 tsp
ground ginger	1 tsp
dessert apples, peeled, cored and coarsely grated	2 medium-sized (yield 200g/2 cups)
raisins or sultanas or golden raisins	75g/½ cup
stem ginger in syrup, drained and chopped	3 pieces
demerara sugar	2 tsp

equipment

20cm (8-inch) shallow square cake tin	Rubber spatula
Parchment/wax paper	Cocktail stick or skewer
2 mixing bowls	Palette (thin, flat-bladed) knife
	Cooling rack

- Pre-heat the oven to 180°C/350°F/Gas Mark 4. Grease the baking tin and line the base with parchment or wax paper. (Lining a baking tin with non-stick baking parchment will make sure you can always turn cakes out successfully.)
- Put the margarine into a mixing bowl, add the fruit sugar and beat with the wooden spoon until it looks smooth, creamy and fluffy, then gradually beat in the eggs.
- In another bowl, mix the flour, baking powder and spices, then add this to the creamed mixture and fold together, using a rubber spatula. Try not to over-mix or the cake could have a heavy texture.
- Stir in the grated apple, sultanas or raisins and chopped stem ginger, then spoon into the prepared tin.
- Level the surface then sprinkle with the sugar. Bake for about 35 minutes until the top is golden. Gently press the surface, the cake should feel firm – test the centre with a cocktail stick or skewer inserted into the middle of the cake. If it comes out clean, the cake is done.
- Cool for 10 minutes then run a palette (thin, flat-bladed) knife around the edge of the cake and turn out onto a wire rack to cool. When completely cool, cut into 12 bars and store in an airtight container.

FROM START TO FINISH: 1 HOUR

chocolate & banana loaf   **SERVES 12**

Perfect to take to the office or offer friends when they drop by for coffee.

good-quality plain/semi-sweet chocolate, 70% cocoa solids	100g/½ cup
ripe bananas	3 medium
light brown Muscavado sugar	50g/⅓ cup
sunflower margarine	50g/¼ cup
eggs	3 medium
plain/all-purpose wholemeal flour	175g/1⅓ cups
baking powder	2 tsp
mixed spice	1 tsp
semi-skimmed milk	3 tbs

equipment

900g/2lb loaf tin	1 large mixing bowl
Parchment/wax paper	Hand-held mixer
1 glass bowl	Spatula
Small saucepan	Cooling rack
2 medium mixing bowls	

- Grease and line the base of the loaf tin with parchment paper. Heat the oven to 180°C/350°F/Gas Mark 4.
- Break the chocolate into a glass bowl, set over a small pan of simmering water until melted. Remove the bowl from the pan and stir the chocolate until smooth.
- Peel the bananas, break into a bowl and roughly mash them.
- Put the sugar into a large bowl, if the sugar is compacted, break it up with your fingertips, add margarine then beat with the hand-held mixer until the mixture looks creamy. Break the eggs into a bowl and beat with a fork, then add to the creamy sugar mixture along with the bananas, melted chocolate, flour, baking powder, mixed spice and milk. Beat until well mixed.
- Using a spatula, transfer the mixture into the tin, level the surface and bake in the oven for 45–50 minutes until risen and a skewer or cocktail stick, inserted into the middle, comes out clean.
- Cool in the tin for 10 minutes before turning out onto a wire rack to cool completely.

FROM START TO FINISH: 1 HOUR

corn fritters with tomato salsa   SERVES 4

These can be eaten as a snack or starter, with or without the salsa. The salsa also makes a great side-dish for grid-dled or barbecued chicken, fish or meat. Any leftover salsa can also be eaten as a snack with wholemeal pitta bread.

To customize the salsa, you can add 2 tbs peeled and finely chopped cucumber and/or half a small green pepper, cut into small dice. For a spicier salsa, add half or a whole red chilli, finely chopped and with seeds removed, or some chopped pickled jalapeños.

tomato salsa

cherry tomatoes or 4 plum or vine tomatoes	225g/1¼ cups or 4
red onion	1 very small
garlic	1 clove
extra virgin olive oil	1 tbs
lemon or lime juice	1 tbs
chopped parsley	1 tbs
salt and freshly ground black pepper	

fritters

sweetcorn	340g/12-oz can
egg	1 large
spring onions/scallions or green onions	2
plain/all-purpose wholemeal flour	40g/⅓ cup
baking powder	½ tsp
milk	3 tbs
extra virgin olive oil	1 tbs

- Make the salsa by cutting the tomatoes in half, squeezing out most of the seeds then chopping the tomatoes into small pieces. Put them into a bowl. Finely chop the onion and peel then very finely chop the garlic. Add to the bowl then stir in the olive oil, lemon juice and parsley. Season with a little salt and pepper.
- Drain the corn, spoon half into the food processor with the egg and process to a thick purée. Scoop into a bowl and add the rest of the corn kernels.
- Finely chop the onions and add to the bowl along with the flour and baking powder and milk. Mix thoroughly.
- Heat the frying pan to medium-high heat, brush with oil then drop 3 tablespoons of the mixture into the pan, leaving space between them to spread.
- Cook for 2–3 minutes until golden underneath, carefully turn them and cook for a further 2 minutes.
- Keep warm in a heated oven or cover with foil while cooking the rest of the fritters, then serve with the tomato salsa.

FROM START TO FINISH: 30 MINUTES

equipment

1 large bowl	Large non-stick frying pan
1 medium bowl	
Food processor or blender	Rubber spatula

1

2

3

4

step-by-step

courgettes

BUYING AND STORING

Known as zucchini in America, courgettes are available all year round. They tend to have a better flavour during the summer months and often small sweeter-flavoured courgettes are available, sometimes with their flowers intact (these are used in some Italian dishes). Courgettes are part of the marrow family. They should have shiny bright green skins with a creamy white-coloured flesh. Check the ends of the courgettes, as they should be moist where they have been cut off the plant. Avoid any that feel light or soft, as this shows they have been stored too long, and do not buy any that are wrinkled or have damaged skins.

Courgettes should be used as soon as possible after buying. If they need to be stored, keep them in the refrigerator as they deteriorate quickly.

HEALTHY BENEFITS

Courgettes have a high water content and provide only small amounts of sugars, dietary fibre, starch and protein. They are low in calories and are therefore useful to use if trying to lose weight. They also contain some potassium, carotene, vitamin C and folic acid but most of these micronutrients are lost when they are fried.

PREPARATION TECHNIQUES

Always start by washing the courgettes. The skin is most often left on but they can be peeled if preferred. A recipe will usually suggest how the courgettes are cut: they can be sliced thinly or thickly; larger ones can be cut in half lengthways then cut into chunks; they can be cut lengthways into batons or fingers; or they can be thinly sliced lengthways into ribbons.

Once prepared, they can be cooked by sautéing, steaming, griddling, microwave cooking or baking. Chunks of courgettes can be threaded onto skewers with other ingredients and cooked under a grill or on a barbecue. Courgettes can be eaten raw and sliced or grated for salads.

TO PREPARE COURGETTES FOR FRITTERS:

1 Wash the courgettes.

2 Top and tail the courgettes/zucchini.

3 Grate on the coarse side of a metal grater.

4 Spread over 3 layers of kitchen paper and sprinkle over with the salt. Roll the courgettes/zucchini up in the paper and set aside for 10 minutes. Squeeze the courgettes/zucchini in the paper to remove the excess water that will have been drawn out of the courgettes/zucchini with the salt. Unroll the paper and transfer the courgettes/zucchini to the bowl.

cornmeal & spring vegetable griddlecakes   **SERVES 8**

These make an excellent eat as a snack with a little ketchup or tomato salsa, or can be served with a salad for a tasty, nutritious light meal.

courgettes/ zucchini, trimmed	450g/1lb
salt	2 tsp
spring onions/scallions or green onions, chopped fine	6
cornmeal (instant polenta)	75g/½ cup
baking powder	1 tsp
cayenne pepper	¼ tsp
ground cumin	½ tsp
egg	1
skimmed milk	150ml/⅔ cup
chopped parsley	2 tbs
freshly ground black pepper	
rapeseed/canola oil	2 tbs

equipment

Grater	Measuring jug or small
Kitchen roll/paper	mixing bowl
towel	Large non-stick frying pan
1 large mixing bowl	Plastic fish slice or spatula

- Grate the courgettes/zucchini (see page 23).
- Trim and finely chop the onions.
- Put the cornmeal, baking powder and spices into a bowl. In a measuring jug or another bowl, beat the egg and milk. Add to the cornmeal mixture and beat.
- Transfer the courgettes/zucchini to the bowl. Add the chopped onions and the parsley and mix together, season with black pepper.
- Heat a large non-stick frying pan, add a tablespoon of the oil then drop 4 large tablespoons of the mixture into the pan. With the back of the spoon level the cakes and press in the mixture from around the edges to give them a neat shape. Cook over a medium heat for about 3–4 minutes. Then, using a plastic fish slice or spatula, carefully turn each cake over to cook for a further 3–4 minutes until golden. Remove from the pan and keep warm, either in a heated oven or covered with foil.
- Reheat the pan, add the remaining oil and cook the rest of the mixture into four more cakes.

FROM START TO FINISH: 35 MINUTES

apricot & oat cookies

SERVES 10

sunflower margarine	115g/½ cup
golden syrup/honey	1 tbs
finely grated orange zest	1 tsp
bicarbonate of soda/ baking soda	1 tsp
hot water	1 tbs
jumbo oats	150g/1½ cups
plain/all-purpose wholemeal flour	75g/⅔ cup
fruit sugar	75g/⅓ cup
dried apricots, small pieces	115g/½ cup

equipment

2 baking sheets	1 small bowl
Grater	1 medium bowl
1 large saucepan	Cooling rack

- Pre-heat the oven to 170°C/325°F/Gas Mark 3; grease the baking sheets.
- Put the margarine, golden syrup and orange zest into a large pan, heat gently until melted. Put the bicarbonate of soda into a small bowl, add the water and, when dissolved, stir into the melted margarine mixture. Mix together the remaining ingredients in a bowl, then tip into the pan and stir well.
- Place in heaped dessertspoonfuls on the baking trays, leaving space between the spoonfuls for the cookies to spread. Bake for 15–20 minutes or until lightly golden. Cool for 2 minutes before transferring to a wire rack.

FROM START TO FINISH: 25 MINUTES

carrot & raisin loaf

SERVES 12

sunflower oil	150ml/⅔ cup
fruit sugar	115g/½ cup
eggs	2 large
unwaxed lemon zest grated fine	1
carrots, peeled and grated	225g/1⅛ cups
raisins or sultanas/ golden raisins	115g/¾ cup
plain/all-purpose wholemeal flour	175g/1¼ cups
bicarbonate of soda/ baking soda	1 tsp
baking powder	1 tsp
mixed spice	1½ tsp

equipment

900g/2-lb loaf tin	1 large mixing bowl
Parchment or wax paper	1 medium mixing bowl
Grater	Skewer or cocktail stick

- Preheat the oven to 180°C/350°F/Gas Mark 4. Grease and line the loaf tin with non-stick parchment/wax paper.
- Put the oil, fruit sugar, eggs and lemon zest into a bowl and beat until the mixture looks smooth. Stir in the grated carrot and raisins.
- Mix together the flour, bicarbonate of soda, baking powder and spice, then fold into the carrot mixture and stir until combined. Spoon into the prepared tin, level the top and bake for 40 minutes until the loaf is risen and golden. Cool in the tin for 10 minutes, then turn out and leave to cool completely on a wire rack.

FROM START TO FINISH: 1 HOUR

marvellous mushrooms **SERVES 2**

chestnut or closed cup mushrooms	225g/2 cups
garlic	1 clove
pinch of salt	
olive oil	1 tbs
granary/ wholegrain bread	2 slices
dried thyme or	¼ tsp
fresh thyme leaves	1 tsp
balsamic vinegar or lemon juice	1 tsp
salt and freshly ground black pepper	to taste

equipment

| Small knife | Large non-stick frying pan |
| Cutting board | Toaster |

- Wipe the mushrooms with kitchen paper, trim the ends of the stalks and cut each mushroom into three thick slices. Peel the garlic (see page 73), place on a board then put the flat blade of the knife on top and press hard to crush the garlic. Add a little salt and with the flat side of the knife, press down and crush further to make a paste.
- Heat a large non-stick pan, then add the oil and mushrooms and cook over a high heat for 3–4 minutes. Toast the bread.
- Add the thyme and garlic to the mushrooms and cook 1 minute more, add the balsamic vinegar and season with a little salt and plenty of black pepper. Serve on the toast.

FROM START TO FINISH: 10 MINUTES

roast garlic & bean dip **SERVES 4**

garlic	1 large head
olive oil	1 tsp
cannellini or butterbeans, rinsed and drained	440g/14-oz can
low-fat soft cream cheese	75g/⅓ cup
lemon juice	1 tbs
extra virgin olive oil	1 tbs
Salt and freshly ground black pepper	
sun-dried tomatoes in oil, chopped fine (optional)	4
raw vegetables: celery hearts, peppers, baby corn, mangetout/snowpeas, radishes, carrots	selection

equipment

| Knife | Sieve |
| Foil | Food processor /blender |

- Pre-heat the oven to 200°C/400°F/Gas Mark 6. Remove the papery outer skin from the head of garlic without separating the cloves. Cut off 1 cm/¼ inch from the stem end. Place on a piece of foil, drizzle over the oil and loosely wrap. Bake for 40 minutes. Leave to cool.
- Squeeze the garlic to remove the cloves from the skins. Put into a blender with the soft cheese, beans, lemon juice and oil. Purée until smooth, then season with salt and pepper. Add the sun-dried tomatoes if desired.
- Serve dip with the vegetables of your choice.

FROM START TO FINISH: 50 MINUTES

1

2

3

4

5

6

step-by-step

chillies

BUYING AND STORING

Chillies can be red or green and belong to the capsicum family of plants. Their strength varies, mostly in relation to their size – they can be long and thin, short and fat or small and round, but generally, the smaller they are the hotter they are. There are hundreds of varieties, but the most readily available are the small, hot bird's eye chillies, used in curries and oriental dishes, or the plump (5cm in length) red or green jalapeno chillies which are much milder and have a fruitier flavour in comparison. Look for any information when purchasing chillies to guide you about their strength.

In some recipes dried chilli flakes are recommended. Flakes are a convenient way of delivering the peppery flavour to a dish.

Look for firm glossy chillies and check the stem looks fresh and green without any trace of mould. Keep fresh chillies in a polythene bag and store them in the refrigerator. They can last up to 2 weeks but this will depend on how fresh they are on purchase. Dried chillies or flakes should be stored in a dark cupboard.

HEALTHY BENEFITS

It is thought that chillies can have a beneficial effect on the heart and circulatory system and also on the respiratory sytem. In addition to containing high levels of the antioxidant capsaicin, they stimulate metabolic rate, relieve congestion and are an aid to digestion.

PREPARATION TECHNIQUES

With their distinctive peppery flavour they certainly add zing to a dish, but most recipes will advise removing the seeds and membranes, as this is where the heat comes from.

1 Start by washing the chillies.

2 Prepare the chillies by cutting off the stalks.

3 Slice through them lengthways.

4 Remove and discard the seeds with a small knife or spoon.

5 Cut into thin strips.

6 Finely chop the strips.

Always wash your hands well after handling fresh chillies as their juice can irritate the skin. Never rub your eyes or touch your face when handling chillies.

chilli & polenta muffins   SERVES 12

Instant polenta or fine cornmeal gives these muffins a distinctive flavour. They are the perfect accompaniment to a salad or barbecue food, and also make a satisfying savoury snack.

white vegetable fat for greasing	1 tsp
fat red chillies	2 large
cloves garlic	2 large
olive oil	3 tbs
self-raising flour or all-purpose flour plus	115g/1 cup
baking soda	1 tsp
baking powder	1 tbs
pinch cayenne pepper	
salt	1 tsp
fine cornmeal or instant polenta	225g/1⅓ cups
Parmesan cheese, finely grated	25g/¼ cup
eggs	2 large
semi-skimmed milk	300ml/1¼ cup

- Preheat the oven to 200°C/400°F/Gas Mark 6. Grease the individual muffin moulds of the tin with vegetable fat.
- Prepare the chillies as shown on page 29. Peel and finely chop the garlic.
- Heat the oil in a small frying pan and cook the chillies and garlic for 2 minutes over a medium-high heat. Remove from the heat and set aside.
- Sieve the flour, baking powder, cayenne and salt into a large bowl, then mix in the cornmeal and Parmesan cheese.
- Beat the eggs and milk together in a jug, then beat in the oil/chillies/garlic mixture. Pour onto the dry ingredients and, using a rubber spatula, mix quickly until just combined.
- Spoon the batter into the muffin tins and bake in the oven for 20 minute until well risen and golden brown. Transfer to a wire rack to cool.

FROM START TO FINISH: 35 MINUTES

chef's tip

If made in advance, these muffins re-heat well in the microwave for 30 seconds.

Make sure you wash your hands and nails thoroughly after preparing the chillies and do not, at any time, rub your eyes. If you have sensitive skin it is best to wear plastic or rubber gloves while slicing the chillies.

equipment

Muffin tin	Sieve
Small frying pan	Measuring jug
Small sharp knife	Rubber spatula
1 large mixing bowl	Cooling rack

raspberry & muesli muffins   **SERVES 12**

You can make these muffins with raspberries, blackcurrants or blueberries. If you use frozen fruit, do not defrost it first or it will go mushy in the batter.

These are best eaten on the day you make them.

self-raising flour or all-purpose flour plus	75g/¾ cup
baking soda	1 tsp
plain/all-purpose wholemeal flour	175g/1⅓ cups
baking powder	1 tbs
fruit sugar	75g/⅓ cup
sugar-free muesli	115g/1¼ cup
skimmed milk	300ml/1¼ cups
egg	1 large
sunflower oil	5 tbs
vanilla extract	1 tsp
fresh or frozen raspberries	150g/1 cup

- Preheat the oven to 200°C/400°F/Gas Mark 6. Place 12 paper muffin cases in the muffin tin.
- Sift the self-raising flour and baking powder into a large bowl, stir in the wholemeal flour, fruit sugar and muesli.
- In a measuring jug beat the milk with the egg, oil and vanilla extract, then add to the dry ingredients. With a large spatula or spoon, quickly and lightly fold together (about 5 turns). Add the raspberries and give the mixture 3 more turns. Do not over-mix. Spoon the batter into the cases.
- Put the tray in the heated oven and bake for 20 minutes until risen and golden. Transfer to a wire rack to cool.

FROM START TO FINISH: 25 MINUTES

equipment

Muffin tin	Measuring jug
Paper muffin cases	Rubber spatula
Large mixing bowl	Cooling rack

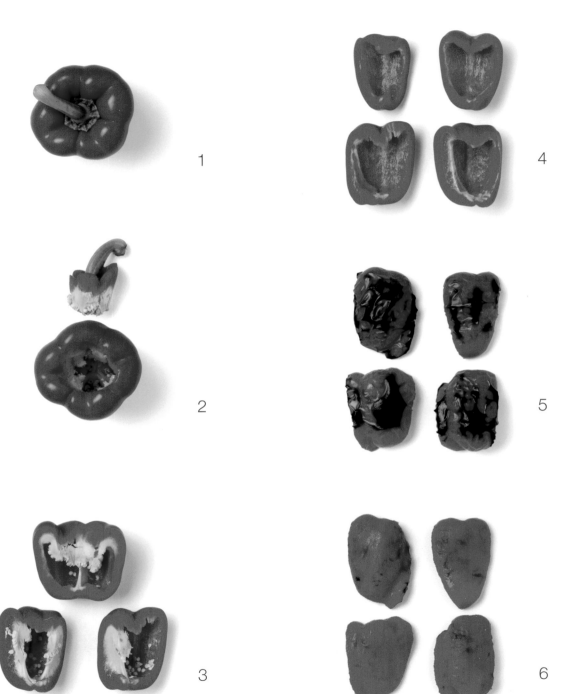

1

2

3

4

5

6

step-by-step

peppers

BUYING AND STORING

Peppers are members of the capsicum family and can be green, red, orange, yellow and black. When buying them, make sure they are firm, bright and smooth; avoid those that are wrinkled or bruised. Store peppers in the refrigerator, where they should keep for a week.

HEALTHY BENEFITS

Peppers are one of the best vegetable sources of Vitamin C, although this is depleted in cooking. The antioxidant action of vitamin C is thought to be improved by flavanoids found in peppers. They are a good source of beta-carotene, the red ones in particular. They also contain traces of vitamins B1 and B2.

For healthy snacks, prepare the peppers by cutting them into strips and serving them with a low-fat dip. Make up a bag of raw vegetable strips to take on a long journey or to the office for a fresh snack full of goodness.

PREPARATION TECHNIQUES

In general, cut the peppers according to their use. They can be sliced, chopped into small or large chunks or diced. They will always need to be deseeded.

1 Start by washing the peppers.

2 Cut a slice off the top, or cut around the stalk with the point of a small knife.

3 Cut the peppers into quarters.

4 Discard the seeds.

5 To skin the peppers, arrange them on a grill pan, skin side up. Place under the grill and cook for about 15 minutes until the skin is evenly charred and blistered.

6 Allow to cool. The skins will now peel off easily and the flesh will be tender.

roast pepper & tomato bruschetta   SERVES 4

These also make a good starter when you're entertaining guests. If you like anchovies, add some – they give the bruschetta a great extra kick.

red peppers	2 medium
plum tomatoes	2
Salt and freshly ground black pepper	
Large pinch caster/ superfine sugar	
thick slices multi-grain or wholemeal bread	4
garlic, halved	1 clove
ricotta cheese	4 tbs
A few basil leaves, shredded	
extra virgin olive oil	2 tsp

- Preheat the grill/broiler. Prepare the peppers as described on page 34.
- While preparing the peppers, slice the tomatoes and place on a plate, seasoning with the salt, pepper and a little sugar.
- Cut the peppers into 1cm/½-inch strips.
- Toast the bread until crisp and golden, then rub one side of each slice with the garlic. Spread on the ricotta cheese, arrange the sliced tomatoes on top, scatter over shredded basil then add the strips of red pepper.
- Drizzle with a few drops of olive oil and a grind or two of black pepper.

FROM START TO FINISH: 20 MINUTES

equipment

Knife   Toaster
Grill pan/broiler

simple salad pizza   SERVES 4

You can top this multi-purpose pizza base with any ingredients you like – peppers, onions, tomatoes, olives, anchovies or even baked beans! If you have run out of bread, this dough is a great substitute: press it out to about 2.5 cm/1-inch thick, score the top into portions and bake it like a large scone, then cut into wedges and serve with soup.

   Instead of the goat's cheese, you can substitute with a crumbly cheese such as Cheshire or Lancashire. Add some slices of roast pepper or some marinated sliced artichokes if you like. Check out the deli counter and try sunblush tomatoes instead of cherry tomatoes or even some roasted baby artichokes.

pizza base

plain/all-purpose wholemeal flour	175g/1¼ cups
oat bran	50g/½ cup
salt	large pinch
baking powder	1 tbs
butter	50g/¼ cup
semi-skimmed milk	120ml/½ cup

topping

pesto sauce	2 tbs
watercress or	1 bunch
rocket	small bag
red onions	2 very small
cherry tomatoes	8
soft goat's cheese	100g/½ cup
extra virgin olive oil	
ground black pepper	

equipment

Baking sheet	Baking parchment/
1 large bowl	wax paper
Cutting board	Cooling rack

- Pre-heat the oven to 200°C/400°F/Gas Mark 6. Grease a baking sheet.
- To make the pizza base put the flour and oat bran into a large bowl with the salt and baking powder. Add the butter, cut it up into small pieces in the bowl, then, using your fingertips, rub it into the flour until crumbly.
- Add enough milk to be able to bring the mixture together to form a soft dough.
- Turn onto a lightly floured board and knead lightly, divide into four pieces and then roll each piece into a ball. Press out to a circle about 10cm/4 inches in diameter.
- Place a piece of non-stick baking parchment on a baking tray, then transfer the rounds of dough on top. Bake in the oven for 8–10 minutes until risen and golden. Cool on a wire rack.
- Spread the tops of the pizza with pesto sauce then add either sprigs of watercress or rocket leaves.
- Peel and slice the red onion and halve the cherry tomatoes and arrange amongst the leaves.
- Break up the goat's cheese and scatter over, then drizzle with a little olive oil. Season with freshly ground black pepper.

FROM START TO FINISH: 25 MINUTES

Whether you work from home or in an office, it's important to stop for lunch to keep energy levels stable. Try to be organized and make soups that will last for two days. Make a large salad to accompany your evening meal and add something extra to the leftovers to give them a new twist for lunch the next day.

lunch on the go

beetroot tabbouleh   **SERVES 4**

Try adding some crumbled feta cheese or a crumbly English cheese such as Cheshire or Lancashire.

This salad actually tastes better if left to stand at least 2 hours or even overnight in the fridge, so it's ideal for making to take to work the next day, by which time the flavours will have fully developed.

bulgur wheat	150g/¾ cup
boiling water	240ml/1 cup
ready-cooked beetroot, drained	250g pack
red onion	½
cucumber	½
chopped parsley	good handful
mint leaves	good handful
extra virgin olive oil	3 tbs
lemon juice	1 tbs
Salt and freshly ground black pepper	

- Put the bulgur wheat into a medium bowl, pour over the water and set aside to soak for 45 minutes until cool and all the water has been absorbed.
- Meanwhile, cut the beetroot and onion into small dice and put into a large bowl.
- Peel the cucumber cut in half lengthways and scoop out the seeds with a teaspoon. Chop the cucumber into small dice and add to the bowl.
- Chop the herbs and add to the bulgur mixture.
- In a small bowl whisk the oil with the lemon juice with a little salt and freshly ground black pepper then add to the salad and fold together. Chill overnight.

FROM START TO FINISH: 1 HOUR

equipment

1 medium bowl	1 small bowl
Knife	Whisk
1 large bowl	

borlotti bean, celery & tomato salad   **SERVES 2**

This dish makes a perfect accompaniment to some simply grilled or broiled fish such as fresh sardines. Alternatively, add some drained canned tuna or prawns.

For a smoother, nuttier flavour, try substituting borlotti beans with butterbeans.

You can buy celery which has already been trimmed and has already had the tougher outside stalks (which are most suitable for cooked dishes) removed. What is left are the sweet hearts, packed and sold in pairs. They are convenient to use, especially for salads and for dips.

celery heart, washed	1
borlotti beans, rinsed and drained	425g/15-oz can
baby plum or cherry tomatoes	225g/1¼ cups
orange or red pepper	1
garlic	1 small clove
extra virgin olive oil	1 tbs
juice of half a lemon	
salt and freshly ground black pepper	
flat leaved parsley finely shredded (optional)	small handful

- Trim a little off the leaf end from the celery heart, and cut across the whole head into thick slices discarding the very end part with the root. Put into a large bowl with the beans.
- Halve the tomatoes, remove the seeds from the pepper and cut into 1 cm/½-inch pieces, then add to the bowl with the tomatoes.
- Place the garlic on a cutting board. Then, with the flat side of a knife, smash to crush, peel away the skin, then add a little salt and crush with the flat side of the knife to make a paste. Put into a small bowl, add the oil and lemon juice, season with pepper and whisk together.
- Pour garlic mixture over the salad and stir in the parsley if using.
- Serve with a granary roll.

FROM START TO FINISH: 10 MINUTES

equipment

Knife	1 small bowl
1 large bowl	Whisk
Cutting board	

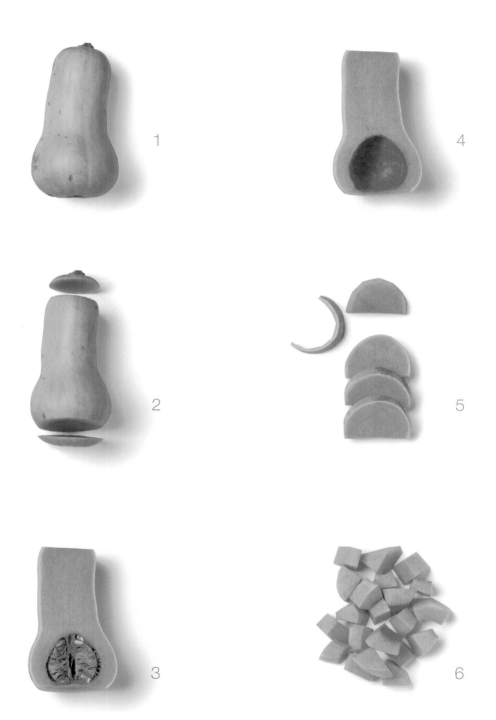

1

2

3

4

5

6

step-by-step

butternut squash

BUYING AND STORING

As part of the squash family, butternut squash is available all year round, unlike the pumpkin and other varieties that are only in season during the autumn and winter months. Their vivid orange flesh livens up many dishes and their sweet nutty flavour complements a variety of other foods. Choose a squash that has a smooth skin and is heavy for its size.

When stored in cool place, butternut squash can keep for several weeks. Once cut, you should remove the seeds and fibres and store in the fridge for no longer than a day, as they will go mouldy very quickly due to their high water content.

HEALTHY BENEFITS

With their wonderful deep-orange colour, they are extremely high in beta-carotene, the antioxidant that helps to ward off many health problems including cancer, heart problems and respiratory disease.

PREPARATION TECHNIQUES

To prepare butternut squash, use a sharp and heavy knife.

1 Start by washing the squash.

2 Cut about 1cm/½-inch slice from the top and bottom.

3 Cut in half lengthways.

4 Scoop out the seeds and stringy fibres from the flesh.

5 Cut the squash into 1cm/½-inch slices (this makes it easier to remove the tough skin) and cut away the skin.

6 Cut into 1cm/½-inch chunks.

classic minestrone   SERVES 4–6

This traditional Italian soup is bursting with vegetables and pulses. It's economical to make, too, and a great way of using up odds and ends of vegetables. Make a big pot, as it will keep for 2 days in the refrigerator.

onion	1 medium
garlic	1 or 2 cloves
celery	3 sticks
carrots	2 medium
olive oil	1 tbs
butternut squash	450g/1lb
vegetable stock	1.8L/7½ cups
chopped tomatoes	225g/8-oz can
sun-dried tomato paste	1 tbs
fine green beans	115g/1¼ cups
cannellini beans	425g/15-oz can
small pasta shapes (e.g. macaroni)	50g/½ cup
salt and freshly ground black pepper	
basil leaves, shredded	small handful
freshly grated Parmesan cheese, to serve (optional)	

equipment	Large saucepan
Vegetable peeler	Sieve
Knife	

- Peel and finely chop the onion and garlic. Trim the celery and cut into small pieces. Peel and cut the carrots into 1cm/½-inch dice.
- Heat the oil in a large saucepan, add the onion and cook over a medium heat for 3–4 minutes to soften, then add the garlic, celery and carrots and cook for 5 minutes.
- Meanwhile, cut the butternut squash into chunks (see page 47), then add to the soup with the stock, canned tomatoes and sun-dried tomato paste. Bring to simmer, cover and cook for 20 minutes.
- While the soup is cooking, trim and cut the green beans into 2.5cm/1-inch lengths. Drain the cannellini beans in a sieve, rinse and drain again. Add the green beans, cannellini beans and the pasta to the soup and simmer for 10 minutes or until the pasta is cooked.
- Season to taste with salt and pepper, then stir the shredded basil. Serve scattered with Parmesan if wished.

FROM START TO FINISH: 45 MINUTES

provençal tomato soup   SERVES 4–6

There are some recipes when canned tomatoes are just more suitable than fresh because they have a reliably full flavour – this is one of those recipes!

red pepper, cut into quarters	1
olive oil	2 tbs
onion, chopped	1 medium
celery, chopped	2 sticks
aubergine/eggplant, diced	1 medium
garlic, chopped fine	2 cloves
plum tomatoes	2 × 395g/14-oz cans
vegetable stock	600ml/2½ cups
sugar	1 tsp
dried basil	1 tsp
salt and freshly ground black pepper, to taste	
fresh basil (optional)	

equipment

Knife   Food processor or
Large saucepan   blender

- Grill/broil the peppers until blistered (see page 35). Meanwhile heat a large pan, add the oil and then the onion and celery. Cook over a medium-high heat for 5 minutes. Set aside.
- Add the aubergine and garlic and stir over a medium-high heat for about 5 minutes more. Stir in the tomatoes, their juices, the stock, sugar and dried basil. Bring to the boil, cover, turn down the heat and cook for 20 minutes.
- Peel the skin from the peppers and cut into small strips or pieces. Remove the soup from the heat; then, in batches, blend to a purée in a food processor or blender. Return to the pan, add the roasted red pepper and reheat. Season if needed. If you would like, add some freshly chopped basil leaves.

FROM START TO FINISH: 45 MINUTES

garden fresh pea & mint soup   SERVES 4

This is a very fresh and zingy soup, especially if you can buy fresh peas in season – though, if not, frozen will do.

leek, trimmed and thinly sliced	1 large
rapeseed/canola oil	1 tbs
onion, chopped fine	1 small
courgettes/zucchini, trimmed and diced	2 medium
garlic, chopped fine	1 clove
vegetable stock	900ml/3¾ cups
fresh (shelled weight) or frozen peas	300g/2 cups
freshly chopped mint	2 tbs
salt and freshly ground black pepper	

- Put all the leek slices in a sieve and give them a good wash under running water to remove any grit. Drain.
- Heat the oil in a large saucepan, add the leek, onion and courgettes and cook over a medium-high heat for 3–4 minutes. Pour in the stock, bring to the boil then turn down the heat, cover the pan and simmer for 15 minutes. Add the peas and cook for 5 minutes more.
- Remove from the heat, uncover, leave to cool for 5 minutes, then add the mint and blend in a food processor or blender until smooth. Season to taste, then reheat before serving.

FROM START TO FINISH: 35 MINUTES

equipment

Knife	Large saucepan
Sieve	Food processor

cauliflower, green bean & tomato salad   **SERVES 4**

This crisp salad can be made and stored in the fridge for up to 2 days. If you prefer, add some chopped anchovies or fried diced bacon or pancetta. The addition of some chopped pitted black or green olives would also enhance the flavours of the other ingredients.

Lightly cooking the cauliflower first will dispel any bitterness and make it more digestible.

cauliflower	1 medium
	(approx 400g/14oz florets
	when prepared)
dwarf beans/string beans	250g/1½ cups
cherry tomatoes	225g/1¼ cups
celery	3 sticks

dressing

extra virgin olive oil	3 tbs
wholegrain mustard	2 tsp
white wine vinegar	1 tbs
salt and freshly ground	
black pepper	
handful parsley leaves,	
thinly shredded	

- Divide the cauliflower into florets, discarding the stalk and cutting any large florets in half so all the pieces are of similar size. Plunge into a pan of boiling salted water for 2–3 minutes, then drain. Tip into a large bowl of cold water, then drain again thoroughly and leave to cool completely.
- As the cauliflower is cooling, trim the beans and cut them in half, then add them to a fresh pan of boiling water. Cook for 4 minutes or until tender, drain and rinse under cold water to cool them and help them keep their fresh green colour.
- Put the cauliflower and beans into a large bowl. Halve the tomatoes and slice the celery thinly. Add to the salad.
- In a small bowl whisk the oil, mustard and vinegar together with a tablespoon of warm water, season to taste then add to the salad and toss together. Scatter in the parsley and serve.

FROM START TO FINISH: 25 MINUTES

equipment

Large saucepan	Small mixing bowl
Colander/strainer	Whisk
2 large mixing bowls	

tuna & crushed chickpea sandwiches   **SERVES 4**

You can use chickpeas that have been soaked overnight and boiled for this sandwich filler, but if you are in a hurry canned ones are just as good. Out of bread? Use tortillas!

chickpeas, rinsed and drained	455g/1-lb can
black olives (stones removed)	8
lemon juice	2 tbs
low-fat Greek-style yogurt	3 tbs
ground cumin	½ tsp
paprika	large pinch
salt and freshly ground black pepper	
tuna in brine	170g/6-oz can
watercress or shredded lettuce	few sprigs
wholemeal seeded bread	8 slices
sunflower margarine	to taste
cherry tomatoes	to serve

- Put the chickpeas, olives, lemon juice, yogurt, cumin, paprika and seasonings to a food processor. Give the machine a few pulses to crush the chickpeas but not to make a purée. (If a food processor is not available, put the chickpeas into a bowl and crush with a fork, cut the stoned olives into small pieces, then mix in the other ingredients.)
- Divide the chickpea mixture between four slices of the bread, add the flakes of tuna and then the sprigs of watercress or shredded lettuce.
- Spread sunflower margarine, if desired, over the remaining slices of bread and cover the sandwiches. Cut in half and serve with some cherry tomatoes.

FROM START TO FINISH: 10 MINUTES

equipment

Sieve	Cherry or olive stoner
Food processor	Knife

mushroom & red pepper sandwiches   **SERVES 4**

This great sandwich filling also doubles as a starter served with toasted rye bread, pitta bread or crackers. Will keep for 2–3 days in the refrigerator.

olive oil	2 tbs
chestnut mushrooms, trimmed and chopped	225g/2 cups
closed cup mushrooms, trimmed and chopped	175g/1¼ cups
garlic, peeled and chopped	1 clove
red pepper, chopped	1
dried thyme	½ tsp
cayenne pepper	⅛ tsp
sunflower seeds or cashew nuts	50g/½ cup
salt and freshly ground black pepper	
seeded or wholegrain bread	8 slices
shredded lettuce	as needed

- Heat a large non-stick frying pan, add the oil then the mushrooms, garlic, red pepper, thyme and cayenne and cook over a high heat, stirring until the mushrooms have softened and the liquid from them has evaporated. Allow to cool for 5 minutes.
- Tip into a food processor, add the sunflower seeds or cashew nuts, then whiz until finely chopped. Season.
- Spread the mushroom mixture over four slices of bread, add a layer of lettuce, then cover with the remaining slices of bread. Wrap with cling film or foil and chill until needed.

FROM START TO FINISH: 20 MINUTES

equipment

Knife	Food processor or blender
1 large frying pan	

spring green coleslaw **SERVES 4–6**

Serve this salad with a sandwich, or add some unsalted peanuts or a mixture of chopped mixed nuts to make it into a complete meal.

Choose pointed spring cabbage for this recipe, as the leaves are sweet while also being crisp.

Ring the changes by adding some freshly chopped mint leaves or a few sprigs of watercress when available.

dressing

natural low-fat yogurt	150g/⅔ cup
extra virgin olive oil	2 tbs
cider vinegar	1 tbs
salt and freshly ground black pepper	

coleslaw

broccoli florets	115g/1 cup
pointed green/hispi cabbage	175g/3 cups
celery heart	1
green pepper	½
bunch spring onions/ scallions or green onions	½

- Put the ingredients for the dressing into a large bowl and whisk together.
- Cut the broccoli into small pieces, using the stalks as well, and put into the bowl.
- Trim off any tough part of the stalk and core from the cabbage and either finely shred the cabbage with a sharp knife or in a food processor. Trim the leaf end from the celery, then cut the stalks into thin slices. Remove the seeds from the pepper and cut into thin slices. Trim the onions and thinly slice.
- Add all the vegetables to the bowl and toss together.

FROM START TO FINISH: 15 MINUTES

equipment

Large bowl
Whisk
Knife

Food processor with shredding blade

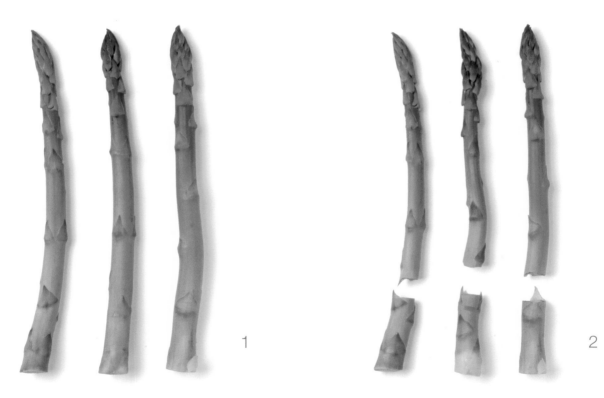

1

2

step-by-step

asparagus

BUYING AND STORING

Asparagus is available all year round, but British-grown asparagus has a short season, from mid-April to the end of June. Look for firm bright green spears, sometimes tinged with purple on the tips. Choose fresh-looking bundles, with tight, undamaged buds and smooth stems; avoid any which look wilted or coarse or that have buds that are beginning to go soft.

There are several different varieties, ranging from thick green, to thin green, fine spruce and white asparagus. Asparagus is best eaten on the day of purchase.

HEALTHY BENEFITS

Asparagus is one of the few vegetables to contain vitamin E and some copper, carotene, vitamin C and folic acid. It is very low in calories 18 kcal/100g, but only when boiled or steamed and not served with butter.

Asparagus is soothing to the urinary tract and wound healing, as well as having mild laxative, sedative and diuretic properties. It has been used for medicinal purposes for hundreds of years.

PREPARATION TECHNIQUES

1 Start by washing the asparagus.

2 To discard the woody ends from the asparagus, hold the stem with both hands and bend until it snaps; it will break where the stem becomes tender.

Cook asparagus either by steaming in a tall narrow pot, especially made for asparagus, or use a vegetable steamer or colander.

To boil asparagus, bring a deep pan containing 2.5cm/ 1 inch of water to the boil. Place the woody ends of the stalks in the water and rest the tips on the sides of the pan. Cook until nearly tender then push the whole of the spears into the water to complete cooking for the final minute or two. The thinner the spears, the shorter the cooking time.

summer rice salad   SERVES 4

The tastes of summer in a salad bowl. To add some protein, toss in some crabmeat or flakes of canned salmon.

brown basmati rice	200g/1 cup
asparagus	250g/9-oz bundle
baby corn	175g/1½ cups
blanched almonds or	75g/1 cup
roasted pumpkin seeds	
red pepper	1
cherry tomatoes	250g/1½ cups
chopped chives	2 tbs

dressing

extra virgin olive oil	2 tbs
lemon juice	1 tbs
pesto sauce	1 tbs
salt and freshly ground	
black pepper	

equipment

Large sieve	Small baking tin
Knife	Large mixing bowl
Large saucepan	Small mixing bowl
Steamer	Whisk

- Place the rice in a sieve and wash under cold running water for 2 minutes. Bring a large pan half full of lightly salted water to the boil, add the rice, turn down the heat to simmer and cook, covered, for 25 minutes or until the rice is tender.
- While the rice is cooking, prepare the asparagus (see page 59). Cut the asparagus into 4cm/1½-inch lengths. Halve or cut the baby corn into thirds (depending on their size). Place vegetables in the steamer over a pan of boiling water; steam for 4 minutes. Remove from the heat, place the steamer under the cold tap and rinse the vegetables to cool quickly. Leave to drain.
- Put the almonds into a small baking tin and place under a grill/broiler for about 2 minutes or until golden, remove and allow to cool, then chop roughly.
- Cut the pepper into quarters and remove the seeds. Cut the cherry tomatoes in half and finely chop the red onion. Put all the prepared vegetables into a large bowl.
- When the rice is cooked, tip into a large sieve and rinse under cold water, then leave to drain. Whisk the dressing ingredients in a small bowl. Add to the vegetables, then add the rice and toss everything together.

FROM START TO FINISH: 45 MINUTES

chef's tip

When fresh asparagus is not in season, use 175g/1½ cups sugar snaps, trimming off the stalks and plunging them into a pan of boiling water for 1 minute. Drain and put into a bowl of cold water to cool quickly, then drain again and cut them in half before adding to the salad.

crispy thai salad   **SERVES 4**

This refreshing, simple salad can be made into a more substantial meal by adding prawns, peanuts or shredded cooked chicken.

carrots	225g/1½ cups
beansprouts, rinsed in cold water	150g/2 cups
red cabbage	175g/3 cups
spring onions/scallions or green onions	4
coriander	small handful

dressing

lime	1
sesame oil	2 tsp
fish sauce	2 tsp
light soy sauce	1 tbs
sugar	1 tsp

- Peel the carrots and cut them into very thin sticks, or pass them through the coarse blade on the grating disc of a food processor. Transfer to a large bowl and add the beansprouts.
- Shred the red cabbage thinly, either with a sharp knife or in the food processor. Trim the onions then cut them into slices on a slant to make pieces about 2.5cm/1 inch in length. Thinly shred the coriander. Add all of these ingredients to the bowl.
- Finely grate the zest of the lime and squeeze out the juice into a small bowl. Add in the rest of the dressing ingredients then whisk together. Pour over the salad, toss together. Cover and refrigerate. Will keep for up to 2 days.

FROM START TO FINISH: 15 MINUTES

equipment

Food processor (optional)	Grater
1 large bowl	Citrus squeezer
1 small bowl	Whisk

sweet potato, carrot & ginger soup   **SERVES 4**

This glowing orange soup is perfect for cold days with its hint of ginger to keep you warm. It's also full of natural vitamins and antioxidants, especially beta-carotene to help protect against illness.

To dress this soup up for entertaining, add a swirl of cream to garnish and a scattering of chopped chives or coriander.

onion	1 medium
garlic	1 clove
fresh ginger	4cm/1½ piece
sweet potatoes	450g/1lb
carrots	400g/3 cups
olive oil	1 tbs
orange or mandarin/ tangerine	1 small
vegetable stock (or 2 stock cubes or liquid/ powdered stock)	900ml/3½ cups
grated nutmeg	large pinch
salt and freshly ground black pepper to taste	

equipment

Vegetable peeler   Large saucepan with lid
Knife   Food processor or blender

- Peel and chop the onion. Peel both the garlic and the ginger and chop both finely. Peel the sweet potatoes and then cut either into chunks or slices. Peel the carrots and cut into thick slices.
- Heat a large pan, add the oil and onion, and cook over a medium-high heat for 3 minutes until beginning to soften. Add the garlic, ginger, prepared sweet potatoes and carrots and stir together. Place the lid on the pan and cook for 5 minutes over a medium-high heat stir twice during cooking.
- Finely grate the rind of the orange. Add to the vegetables, then pour in the stock. Bring to the boil, cook over a low-medium heat for 25 minutes or until the vegetables are very soft.
- Remove from the heat, uncover and cool for 5 minutes, then purée in a food processor or blender – you will have to do this in two batches.
- Return the soup to the pan, add the nutmeg and season with salt and pepper, if needed.

FROM START TO FINISH: 40 MINUTES

1

2

3

4

step-by-step

onion

BUYING AND STORING

There are several varieties of onion, ranging from the mild Spanish onion; yellow onions with a brown skin, which are used mostly in everyday cooking; red onions, which have a sweet flavour that means they are delicious raw or cooked; and small shallots, which have a purple-tinged flesh and a more intense, sweeter flavour than onions. Generally, the smaller the onion, the stronger the flavour.

Look for onions that are firm and in good condition and have tight shiny skins. They should not show signs of being mouldy or soft. Avoid onions that are sprouting, as they will be soft inside. Onions should be stored in a cool dry place, preferably in a brown paper bag to prevent them sprouting. They can be kept for weeks in the right conditions, but should not be kept in a warm kitchen for more than a few days.

HEALTHY BENEFITS

This vegetable is a powerful natural antibiotic, and has been used for hundreds of years to kill many disease-causing bacteria. It helps the body's metabolism by lowering cholesterol, blood fat and blood sugar. It also assists in 'thinning' the blood to minimize the risk of clotting. Onions contains flavanoids and sulphurs, which may even help to fight cancers. They also contain a little calcium and folic acid. Furthermore, the onion is the richest dietary source of quercetin, a potent antioxidant and sedative.

PREPARATION TECHNIQUES

Onions can be prepared in many different ways. Once peeled, a recipe may require it to be sliced, chopped, grated or even puréed to be used in a marinade.

1 Start with a nice firm onion.

2 Cut a small slice off the top of the onion and peel away the skin.

3 Cut in half and place on a board, cut-side down. Cut thin slices from the root end to the top.

4 Now cut across the slices to make small dice. Discard the root.

TIP

The sharper and finer the blade of the knife, the easier it is to avoid breaking the shape of the onion as it is sliced. This will stop it slipping under your fingers.

chicken, spinach & new potato salad **SERVES 4**

A fresh-tasting salad with a great mix of flavours and textures. Add some flakes of freshly-shaved Parmesan cheese if you like.

new potatoes	450g/1lb
red onion, finely chopped	1
olive oil	1 tbs
skinless chicken breasts, cut into thin strips	500g/1lb 2oz
baby leaf spinach	175g/3 cups
chopped parsley	

dressing

extra virgin olive oil	3 tbs
lemon juice	2 tbs
wholegrain mustard	2 tsp
sugar	pinch
salt and freshly ground black pepper	to taste

- Cut the potatoes into halves or quarters, depending on their size. Try to have them all of equal size. Cook the potatoes in a pan of salted water for 12–15 minutes until tender, then drain. Transfer to a large bowl.
- Meanwhile, whisk the dressing ingredients together in a small bowl, seasoning with salt and pepper. Chop the onion as shown on page 67.
- Heat a large non-stick frying pan, add the olive oil and the chicken and cook for 4–5 minutes stirring until the chicken is golden brown and not pink if you cut through a strip. Tip into the bowl with the potatoes.
- Add the spinach, onion and dressing and toss together then divide between four plates.
- Scatter over the parsley and serve.

FROM START TO FINISH: 25 MINUTES

equipment

Large saucepan	1 small bowl
Colander or strainer	Large non-stick frying
1 large bowl	pan

Here are some great ideas for dishes that are both quick to cook and economical. A well-stacked cupboard can provide a variety of healthy ingredients to make easy mid-week meals.

dinners fast & fresh

1

4

2

5

3

6

step-by-step

garlic

BUYING AND STORING

Dried garlic, with which we are most familiar, is available all year round. Fresh garlic is available from June to October. The bulbs are made up of small sections known as cloves and they are held together with a papery covering. The cloves can vary in size, so judgement needs to be exercised when deciding how much to use. Look for bulbs that are heavy for their size and show no signs of sprouting.

Keep unwrapped in a cool dark place for up to 2–3 weeks or store in the refrigerator for up to a month.

HEALTHY BENEFITS

Garlic contains allicin, which is antibiotic and antifungal and boosts the immune system, and sulphides, which may even help prevent cancers, and an antioxidant, which lowers blood cholesterol and prevents clotting. Garlic also fights various gastro-intestinal infections.

PREPARATION TECHNIQUES

Garlic is usually crushed before it is used, although in some recipes, finely chopped or sliced is more suitable. Whichever way it is prepared, it should never be added to onion to cook for a long time as it will burn and taste bitter. Garlic only needs to be fried for 30 seconds to 1 minute.

1 Start with a fresh bulb.

2 Separate the required number of cloves from the bulb.

3 Place the garlic on a cutting board. Smash the garlic with the flat side of a knife.

4 Peel away the skin.

5 If there is a green sprout in the centre, remove it, as it can taste bitter.

6 Add a little salt and crush the garlic with the flat side of the blade to make a paste.

cumin-scented lamb chops with sweet potato mash   **SERVES 4**

The sweet potato mash is almost a meal in itself: you could serve it topped with some grilled/broiled bacon and a poached egg for a different meal. Serve with a green vegetable such as broccoli, spinach or green beans.

thick loin lamb chops	4
garlic	1 large clove
olive oil	1 tbs
cayenne pepper	¼ tsp
paprika	½ tsp
ground cumin	1 tsp
lemon juice	2 tsp
salt and freshly ground black pepper	

sweet potato crush

white potatoes	200g/7oz
sweet potatoes	2 large (approx 600g/1½lb)
butter	25g/2 tbsp/¼ stick
chilli flakes	large pinch
spring onions/scallions or green onions, trimmed and chopped	5

equipment

Sharp knife	Large saucepan
Small bowl	Frying pan
Pastry brush	

- With a sharp knife trim off any excess fat from the edge of the chops, and place them on a plate. Peel and crush the garlic (see page 73). Mix with the oil, spices and lemon juice and then brush the chops with this mixture on both sides, and season with salt and pepper. If time permits allow to marinate in the fridge for half an hour; if not, proceed.

- Cut the potatoes into equal-sized chunks. Put the white potatoes in a pan of cold water with a little salt, bring to the boil and cook for 5 minutes. Add the sweet potatoes and cook for approximately 10 minutes more, or until all the potatoes are tender.

- Meanwhile place the chops under a medium-hot grill/broiler for about 5 minutes on each side until golden and cooked through.

- Heat the butter with the chilli flakes in a small frying pan, add the onions and simmer for 2 minutes. Remove from the heat.

- Drain the potatoes and return to the pan, break up with a fork, then add the onion mixture. Keep the texture chunky. Season if needed.

- Serve the lamb chops with the potatoes.

FROM START TO FINISH: 30 MINUTES

cook's tips

- If you like your lamb chops a bit pink, cook for 4 minutes on each side, though this will depend on their thickness. Test with a metal skewer and look at the juices to make sure the chops are cooked to your liking.

pasta with grilled tomatoes, red onion & celery **SERVES 4**

penne pasta	250g/1¾ cups
cherry tomatoes	500g/3 cups
celery heart	1
olive oil	2 tbs
red onions, chopped	2 medium
salt and freshly ground black pepper	
dry white wine	120ml/½ cup
basil leaves, shredded	handful
pinenuts, toasted	25g/¼ cup

- Put the pasta to cook in a large pan of salted boiling water for 10–12 minutes. Halve the tomatoes and place on a foil-lined grill/broiler rack and brush with half of the oil. Season, then place under the grill/broiler for about 5 minutes until golden. Meanwhile cut the celery into 5mm/¼ inch slices.
- Heat the rest of the oil in a large frying pan, cook the onions for 2–3 minutes over a medium-high heat, then add the celery and cook for a further 4–5 minutes. Pour over the wine and turn the heat to high, cooking until the wine has almost evaporated. Tip the tomatoes and their juice into the pan.
- Drain the pasta and gently fold into the vegetables with the basil. Serve scattered with pinenuts.

FROM START TO FINISH: 25 MINUTES

equipment

1 large saucepan	Grill/broiling pan
Sharp knife	Large non-stick frying pan

quick fish & pasta pie **SERVES 4**

leek, trimmed and cut into medium-thick slices	1 medium
olive oil	2 tbs
plain/all-purpose flour	25g/¼ cup
dry white wine	150ml/⅔ cup
vegetable stock	150ml/⅔ cup
single cream	142ml/5-fl oz carton
thick cod fillet, cubed	350g/12oz
frozen peas	175g/1½ cups
salt and ground pepper	
peeled prawns	175g/1½ cups
shaped pasta, cooked	150g/1 cup
tomatoes, sliced	5

- Put the sliced leek in a sieve and give a good wash under running cold water to remove any grit. Drain. Heat the oil in the pan, add the leek and cook for 3–4 minutes. Stir in the flour, then gradually add the wine and the stock. Stirring all the time, bring to simmer and cook for 3 minutes. The sauce should be quite thick. Stir in the cream.
- Add the cod and peas and cook for 5 minutes, gently turning the mixture so the fish cooks evenly. Season with a little salt and pepper, add the prawns and drained pasta, heat through for a minute. Spoon into an ovenproof dish.
- Arrange the sliced tomatoes on top, then place under a pre-heated grill/broiler and cook for 10 minutes until the tomatoes are lightly browned.

FROM START TO FINISH: 35 MINUTES

equipment

1 medium saucepan	Large deep frying pan or
Sharp knife	sauté pan
Sieve	Shallow ovenproof dish

kale frittata   SERVES 4

Curly kale is an invaluable vegetable, highly nutritious and rich in vitamins, minerals and phytochemicals that guard against infections, heart disease and cancer.

olive oil	3 tbs
kale, trimmed, steamed and chopped	200g/2 cups
onion, sliced fine	1 medium
garlic, crushed	2 cloves
eggs, beaten	6 large
grated Parmesan	4 tbs
salt and pepper	to taste

- Heat half of the oil in a medium frying pan, add the onion and garlic and cook gently for 10 minutes, stirring or until soft and golden. Pour out into a bowl and add the kale, eggs, cheese and seasonings.
- Pour the remaining oil into the pan and place over a medium-high heat. Add the kale mixture, then, as soon as it begins to set, loosen it a little around the edges. Continue to cook over a low heat for about 8 minutes until the egg has almost set. Meanwhile, heat the grill/broiler.
- Pop under the hot grill/broiler for 2 minutes until the top is golden. Cut into wedges and serve warm or cold.

FROM START TO FINISH: 30 MINUTES

equipment

Steamer	23cm/9-inch non-stick frying pan
Mixing bowl	
Measuring jug	

cheeky turkey chilli   SERVES 4

rapeseed/canola oil	1 tbs
onion, finely chopped	1 medium
turkey mince	500g/1lb 2oz
garlic, chopped fine	2 cloves
red or green pepper, chopped	1
red or green chilli, chopped	1
cumin powder	1 tsp
medium/hot chilli powder	1 tsp
chopped tomatoes	400g/14-oz can
tomato purée/paste	1 tbs
chicken stock	150ml/⅔ cup
dried oregano	1 tsp
red kidney beans, rinsed and drained	400g/14-oz can
salt and freshly ground black pepper	to taste

- Heat a large non-stick deep frying pan, add the oil and onion and cook for 2 minutes until it begins to soften. Stir in the turkey mince and continue to cook for 5 minutes or until the turkey is lightly browned.
- Add the garlic, pepper and chilli with the spices and cook for 1 minute, then stir in the canned tomatoes, tomato purée, stock and oregano. Bring to simmer, cover with a lid and cook for 20 minutes.
- Add the beans to the turkey mixture; season. Cook for a further 5 minutes. Serve with cooked basmati rice.

FROM START TO FINISH: 45 MINUTES

equipment

1 large, deep non-stick frying pan or sauté pan with lid	Knife
	Sieve

aromatic vegetable korma   **SERVES 4**

Although coconut milk has a high GI rating, this will be balanced by all the low-GI vegetables in this recipe. You can buy reduced-fat coconut milk and, in this recipe, spray oil is used to compensate for the fat in the coconut milk.

onion	1 medium
sweet potatoes	2–3 (approx 650g/1lb 6 oz)
cauliflower	1 medium
basmati rice	175g/1 cup
spray oil	
garlic	1 clove
medium curry paste	2 tbs
vegetable stock	250ml/1 cup
reduced-fat coconut milk	400ml/14-oz can
flat green or runner beans	250g/1½ cups
frozen peas	115g/¾ cup
cornflour	1 tsp
water	1 tbs
chopped coriander or parsley (optional)	

equipment

Knife	Large saucepan
Medium saucepan	Sieve

- Chop the onion, then peel and cut the sweet potatoes into 2.5cm/1-inch chunks. Divide the cauliflower up into florets, cutting any large ones in half so they are all roughly the same size.
- Put the basmati rice to cook in a medium pan of slightly salted boiling water for 10–12 minutes until tender.
- Heat a large pan, add the oil and onion and cook over a medium heat for 5–8 minutes until golden. Add the garlic and curry paste and, when blended into the onions, add the sweet potatoes and stock then bring to simmer and cook for 5 minutes.
- Add the cauliflower and coconut cream, cover and simmer for 6–8 minutes, stirring from time to time for even cooking.
- By this time the sweet potatoes and cauliflower should be getting tender. Trim the beans, remove the strings from the side and cut into 4 cm/1½-inch pieces. Add to the pan along with the peas and cook, uncovered, for 5 minutes, stirring so all the vegetable are evenly cooked.
- Blend the cornflour and water, stir into the curry and cook 1–2 minutes until the sauce thickens slightly.
- Drain the rice and serve the curry on a bed of rice scattered with chopped herbs if wished.

FROM START TO FINISH: 35 MINUTES

mandarin chicken stir-fry **SERVES 4**

This dish has a subtle sweet and sour taste that is not as pronounced as that of the take-aways and ready meals available.

The secret about cooking stir-fries is to prepare all the ingredients before you start cooking, as once that wok is hot, it's fast and furious on the stove.

Serve with boiled basmati rice or cooked noodles.

spring onions/scallions or green onions, chopped	1 bunch
red pepper, diced	1
garlic, chopped fine	2 cloves
red or green chilli, seeded (optional), chopped fine	1
mandarin oranges (finely grated zest and juice)	2
rice vinegar	2 tsp
honey	2 tsp
cornflour	1 tsp
vegetable oil	2 tbs
skinless chicken breasts, diced	500g/1lb 2oz
dark soy sauce	3 tbs
sweetcorn niblets, drained	340g/12-oz can
water	5 tbs

- Chop the white part of the onions into 2.5cm/1-inch lengths, then slice the green part and put to one side. Put the white part of the onions, pepper, garlic and chilli into a bowl.
- Put the mandarin juice into a bowl with the vinegar, honey and cornflour and blend together.
- Heat a wok or large non-stick frying pan, add 1 tbs of the oil and then the chicken, and stir-fry until just golden. Add the soy sauce and toss together, then tip out into a bowl.
- Put the remaining oil in the pan, add the onions, peppers, garlic and chilli and stir-fry together for 3 minutes. Return the chicken to the pan with the drained sweetcorn, mandarin zest and the blended ingredients, plus the water. Allow to bubble up for 1 minute to thicken. Scatter over the sliced green onions.

FROM START TO FINISH: 20 MINUTES

equipment

Sharp knife	Large frying pan
2 chopping boards	or wok
3 medium bowls	Measuring jug

1

2

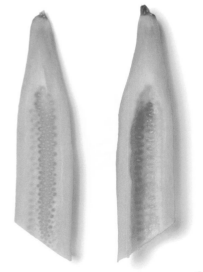

3

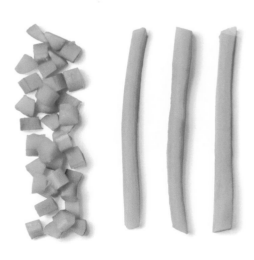

4

step-by-step

cucumber

BUYING AND STORING

Cucumbers are available all year round and are most often used in salads and sandwiches. They can also be made into soup. When buying a cucumber, look for a firm one and avoid any that are slightly yellowed or have a wrinkled skin and soft ends. Cucumbers are mostly sold in a tight plastic wrapping. Uncut, they will keep in the refrigerator for up to 5 days; cut, they will keep for 2 days.

HEALTHY BENEFITS

Cucumbers have a very high water content. They also contain folic acid and some potassium and vitamin C. They are mildly diuretic.

PREPARATION TECHNIQUES

Cucumber can be peeled or not as required.

1 Start with a fresh piece of cucumber, cut to the length you require.

2 Peel the cucumber.

3 Cut in half lengthways and scoop out the seeds with a teaspoon.

4 Cut into thin strips and then chop into small dice.

moroccan lamb burgers   SERVES 4

These make a nice change from beef burgers; the addition of the bulgur wheat gives them a new twist. They can be barbecued, griddled or grilled/broiled.

bulgur wheat	50g/¼ cup
onion, roughly chopped	1 small
garlic, finely chopped	2 cloves
chopped parsley or coriander	2 tbs
ground coriander	2 tsp
ground cumin	1 tsp
ground cinnamon	½ tsp
minced lamb	500g/1lb 2oz
salt and freshly ground black pepper	to taste
A little oil	

cucumber & mint yogurt

low-fat Greek-style plain yogurt	150g/⅔ cup
cucumber	115g/¾ cup
chopped fresh mint	1 tbs

- Put the bulgur wheat into small pan, cover with hot water and boil for 10 minutes. Drain, rinse with cold water and drain again
- Meanwhile, put the yogurt into a small bowl. Cut the cucumber into small dice (see page 83) and add to the yogurt with the mint.
- Transfer the bulgur wheat to a food processor, add the onion, garlic and parsley and whiz until finely chopped. Add the spices, lamb and seasoning and pulse until just mixed together. With wet hands, shape the mixture into 4 or 8 smaller burgers.
- Prepare the barbecue, grill/broiler or griddle for cooking the burgers. Brush the rack with a little oil and cook the burgers for 5–6 minutes on each side until cooked through.
- If cooking on a griddle pan, lightly brush the burgers before putting them on the hot pan. Serve with the cucumber salad.

FROM START TO FINISH: 35 MINUTES

equipment

1 small saucepan	Barbecue, grill/broiler
Sieve	or griddle pan
1 small bowl	Pastry brush
Food processor	

salmon kedgeree   SERVES 4

This is a quick dish to put together if you have some cooked basmati rice in the fridge. If planning meals ahead, cook extra with this dish in mind.

basmati rice	225g/1¼ cups
salmon fillets	2 (approx 350g/12oz)
bay leaf	1
eggs	2 large
leek	1 large (approx 225g/8oz)
butter	25g/2 tbs/¼ stick
curry powder	2 tsp
low-fat crème fraiche	3 tbs
salt and freshly ground	
black pepper	
chopped chives or parsley	3 tbs

equipment

Medium saucepan	Sieve
Frying pan with lid	Knife
Small saucepan	

- Cook the rice in a pan of boiling slightly salted water for 10–12 minutes until tender. While the rice is cooking put the salmon into a deep frying pan, cover with water, add the bay leaf and bring to the boil. Turn down the heat immediately, cover the pan and poach gently for 5 minutes, then leave to stand for 5 minutes.
- In a separate small pan, boil the eggs for 6 minutes, drain and run under cold water, then remove the shells. Drain the rice. Lift the salmon out of the pan and onto a plate, flake the fish into large pieces and discard the skin. Wash the frying pan.
- Trim the top part and root end of the leek, discard the outer layer, cut lengthways in half and then again lengthways, chop into 1cm/½-inch pieces, put any gritty bits from the green end into a sieve and rinse under cold a cold tap. Drain.
- Heat the frying pan, add the butter and, when melted, add the leek and cook over a medium heat for 3–4 minutes until softened. Stir in the curry powder; cook briefly. Stir in the rice and crème fraiche and, when fully coated with the spices, add the salmon to the pan and season.
- Heat together, gently turning the ingredients.
- Finally, chop the eggs and add to the kedgeree with the chives, gently fold together and serve.

FROM START TO FINISH: 20 MINUTES

warm puy lentils with leeks & goat's cheese   **SERVES 4**

Learn to love lentils – they are rich in nutrients and an excellent low-GI food. Puy lentils are quick to cook and do not need soaking. They can be eaten warm or cold as a salad with the little dressing added and mixed with salad leaves. Choose feta cheese if you prefer it to goat's cheese.

carrot	1 large
stalk celery	1 large
puy lentils	250g/1¼ cups
bay leaf	1
thyme or	3 sprigs
dried thyme	1 tsp
extra virgin olive oil	3 tbs
onion	1 small
garlic	1 large clove
leeks	2 medium
	(approx 350g/12oz)
tomatoes	2
balsamic vinegar	1 tbs
salt and freshly ground	
black pepper	
freshly chopped parsley	3 tbs
soft goat's cheese	115g/4-oz pack

- Peel the carrot and cut into small dice. Trim the celery and finely chop.
- Put the lentils into a sieve and run under cold water, then put into a large saucepan with the carrot, celery and herbs, and cover with cold unsalted water. Bring to the boil. Cover the pan and cook for about 15–20 minutes until just tender.
- Meanwhile, peel and chop the onion, and finely chop the garlic. Top and tail the leeks to remove the course upper leaves and lower root, and cut into medium-thick slices. Put the green parts in a sieve and give a good wash under running cold water to remove any grit.
- To skin the tomatoes, see page 119. Roughly chop.
- Heat 1 tbs of the olive oil in a medium non-stick frying pan, add the onions and cook 2–3 minutes until beginning to soften, then add the sliced leeks and garlic and stir-fry for 5 minutes until just tender.
- Drain the lentils, discard the bay leaf and sprigs from the thyme and put into a medium bowl.
- In a small bowl, whisk the extra virgin olive oil and vinegar together with a little salt and pepper. Add to the lentils with the leeks, tomatoes and parsley and toss together. Divide between four serving plates, topping each serving with the crumbled goat's cheese.

FROM START TO FINISH: 35 MINUTES

equipment

Vegetable peeler	Medium non-stick frying pan
Sharp knife	1 medium bowl
Sieve	1 small bowl
Large saucepan	Whisk

Home alone shouldn't mean ready meals in front of the TV. These recipe ideas will inspire you to make delicious meals for yourself even if you are the most reluctant cook.

There are suggestions on how to capitalize on your cooking time that provide you with the basis of another creation for the next day.

just for one

cabbage, potato & bacon pan fry   **SERVES 1**

This is a great brunch idea, and could be made with some cold boiled new potatoes left over in the fridge.

small new potatoes	125g/¾ cup
Savoy cabbage	115g/2 cups
1 tbs sunflower oil	1 tbs
onion	1 small
thick cut rashers	2 (approx 100g/3½oz)
unsmoked bacon	
Worcestershire sauce	2 tsp

equipment

Small saucepan with steamer	Large non-stick frying pan

- Cut the potatoes in half and if necessary into quarters to give chunks about 2.5cm/1 inch in size. Put into a pan of lightly salted water, bring to the boil and cook for 3 minutes during which time cut the cabbage into shreds 1 cm/½ inch wide and place in a steamer. Place on top of the potatoes and cook together for 4 minutes. Drain the potatoes.
- Meanwhile, slice the onion thinly and cut the bacon into thin strips, Heat a large non-stick frying pan, add the oil then the onion and bacon and cook for 5 minutes over a medium-high heat. Add the potatoes and continue to cook for a further 5 minutes until all the ingredients are turning golden.
- Lower the heat, add the cabbage with the Worcestershire sauce and cook for 1 minute until heated through. Season if needed.

FROM START TO FINISH: 25 MINUTES

1

2

3

4

step-by-step

mackerel

BUYING AND STORING

Mackerel is a long, slender fish with blue-black markings on its back. The flesh is creamy coloured and it has a very distinctive flavour. It is mostly sold whole and can be cooked whole or filleted.

When buying mackerel, or fish in general, always look for firm fish with smooth skin and bright eyes and avoid fish that is wrinkled or has a dry skin. Fish is very perishable and should be stored in the coldest part of the refrigerator. It should be cooked and eaten within 24 hours of purchase.

HEALTHY BENEFITS

A fatty fish, mackerel provides protein and is a good source of omega-3 polyunsaturated fatty acids, which help to prevent heart disease and stroke and may even help to prevent some cancers and minimize the symptoms of arthritis. It is also provides well-absorbed iron, vitamin A and B12, potassium, selenium, copper, zinc, vitamin D, niacin, vitamin B6, riboflavin, pantothenic acid and biotin. One small mackerel provides the full daily requirement of iodine, which is essential for a healthy thyroid gland and regulating metabolic rate.

PREPARATION TECHNIQUES

1 Start with a whole mackerel.

2 Cut the head, tail and fins off the fish. Wash the inside and remove any remains of blood.

3 Place the mackerel on a board and make sure it is cut through right down to the end of the tail. Turn it onto its cut side and gently press down the bone to flatten the fish.

4 Turn the fish over and wipe away any grey membranes near to where the gills were. Lift the bone from the head end and carefully peel it away from the flesh.

lemon-grilled mackerel on butterbean purée   **SERVES 1**

Mackerel is inexpensive and a terrific source of Omega 3 oils. The lemon juice cuts through the richness of the fish, and the purée, made with low-GI butterbeans, makes a great alternative to mashed potato.

mackerel	1
shallot	1
garlic	1 small clove
butter	small knob
butterbeans, drained and rinsed	225g/8-oz can
lemon (juice)	½
well-flavoured vegetable stock	3 tbs
low-fat Greek-style yogurt	2 tbs
salt and freshly ground black pepper	
olive oil	½ tsp
lemon	½
medium oatmeal	1 tbs
chopped parsley	

equipment

Grill/broiling pan

- Prepare the mackerel as described on page 95.
- Finely chop the shallot and garlic very finely. Heat a small pan, add the butter and when melted, add the shallot and garlic and cook for 2 minutes, until softened. Add the beans, lemon juice and stock and toss together to heat through 3–4 minutes. Tip into a food processor or blender, add the yogurt and whiz to make a thick purée. Season if needed. Using a rubber spatula, turn back into the pan.
- Line the rack of the grill/broiling pan with foil, brush with oil then lay the fish on the foil, skin side up, and brush with oil. Place under a medium-hot grill/broiler about 5cm/2 inches away from the source of heat and cook for 2–3 minutes. Turn the fish over and season lightly.
- Finely grate the lemon zest and mix with the oatmeal then scatter evenly over the fish and pat down lightly. Return to the grill/broiler and cook for a further 3 minutes or until golden.
- Reheat the butterbean purée. Spoon onto a warm plate and lift the fish on top. Cut the fish into two fillets if preferred. Scatter over a little chopped parsley.

FROM START TO FINISH: 15–20 MINUTES

chef's tips

- Make sure the mackerel is really fresh, the eyes should be clear and the skin firm and glistening. Ask the fishmonger to fillet the fish to save time.
- Try trout if mackerel is not in season.
- For a small quantity of stock, use either a liquid concentrate or a powdered stock to mix with hot water.

barley risotto with butternut squash   **SERVES 1**

Pearl barley, with its low GI, is used here instead of Arborio rice. Can be eaten cold for lunch the next day, so maybe double the ingredients.

olive oil	1 tbs
shallot, chopped fine	1
garlic, chopped fine	1 small clove
butternut squash (see page 47)	175g/1⅛ cups
vegetable stock	450ml/2 cups
pearl barley	50g/¼ cup
white wine	splash
ripe tomato, skinned and chopped (see page 119)	1 medium
sage leaves, finely chopped	6
salt and freshly ground black pepper	
Parmesan cheese, freshly grated	10g/2 tbs

- Heat the oil in a medium-sized pan, add the shallot and garlic and cook over a gentle heat for 2 minutes. Add the squash and turn in the oil over a low heat for 2 minutes. If the squash is sticking, add a little stock. Stir in the barley and wine and allow to bubble up, then stir in the tomato and sage.

- Pour in a third of the stock and stir over a medium heat until it is absorbed (about 5 minutes). Add the remaining stock and continue to simmer, uncovered, stirring from time to time for 25 minutes until all the stock is absorbed and the barley is tender. The risotto should have a creamy texture and the squash will be very tender and partially broken up. Season, add the Parmesan and turn into a bowl.

FROM START TO FINISH: 45 MINUTES

equipment

Medium-sized pan

lemon dhal with spinach   SERVES 1

Make double the quantity of the dhal and, with the second half, add enough vegetable stock to make a soup, whiz in a food processor or blender. Perfect for lunch the next day.

sunflower oil	2 tsp
onion	1 medium-small
split red lentils, rinsed	75g/½ cup
turmeric	¼ tsp
water	300ml/1¼ cups
lemon	½ small
(grated zest and juice)	
mild curry paste	1 tsp
baby spinach leaves	75g/1¼ cups
salt and freshly ground	
black pepper	

equipment

Medium saucepan   Small frying pan

- Chop finely about one-third of the onion, heat 1 teaspoon of the oil in a medium-sized saucepan, add the onion and cook for 2–3 minutes over a medium heat. Add the lentils, turmeric and water. Cover and simmer for 25–30 minutes, adding a little more water if needed. The lentils should be soft and well cooked.

- Meanwhile, thinly slice the remaining onion. Heat a small frying pan, add the oil and cook the onion over a medium-high heat, moving them around the pan with a wooden spoon for about 5 minutes, until golden and crisp.

- Stir the curry paste and spinach into the lentils and cook for about 3 minutes until the spinach has wilted. Season with salt and pepper then spoon the dhal into a bowl and top with the crispy onions. Serve with a chopped tomato and coriander salad.

FROM START TO FINISH: 40 MINUTES

griddled chicken with patatas bravas   SERVES 1

Make double the amount of potatoes, add some diced ham and fresh halved cherry tomatoes to make a salad for lunch the next day. If you find Spanish smoked paprika in the supermarket, use it in this recipe to give it a smoky flavour.

skinless chicken breast	1
Italian mixed herbs	½ tsp
Olive oil for brushing	

potatoes

small new potatoes	75g/½ cup
olive oil	1 tsp
onion	½ small
garlic	1 small clove
tomatoes	2
tomato purée/paste	1 tsp
dried chilli flakes	good pinch
paprika	½ tsp
sugar	pinch
salt and freshly ground	
black pepper	
chopped parsley	

equipment

Small saucepan   Griddle pan
Small frying pan

- Put the potatoes into a pan of water and bring to the boil, cook for 10–12 minutes until almost tender, drain.
- While the potatoes are cooking, cut the chicken through horizontally about three-quarters the way then open out the breast like a book and flatten it with the palm of the hand. Brush with oil and scatter over the herbs, season lightly and set aside. Chop the onion and garlic finely and skin the tomatoes (see page 119) and chop finely. Cut the potatoes into 2.5cm/1-inch cubes.
- Heat the olive oil in a small non-stick frying pan, add the onion and garlic and cook for 2 minutes over a medium heat. Stir in the chopped tomatoes, purée, chilli flakes, paprika, sugar and 4 tbs water. Cook.
- During this time cook the chicken. Heat a griddle pan and when hot place the chicken in the pan, cook for 6–8 minutes, turning half-way.
- Stir the potatoes into the tomato sauce and heat through, season if needed and spoon onto a plate, scatter over the parsley then place the chicken on top.
- Serve with a green salad.

FROM START TO FINISH: 30 MINUTES

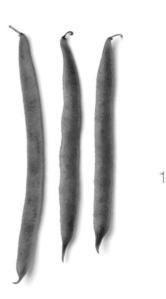

1

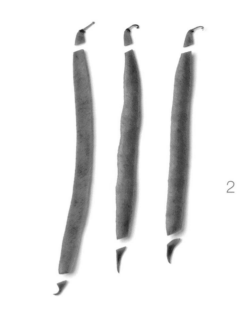

2

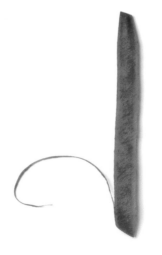

3

4

step-by-step

runner beans

BUYING AND STORING

Also called string beans, runner beans are available from July to September/October. Try to choose slender firm pods without any developing seeds. If they are lumpy and the skins feel rough they were left too long to grow and will be tough and stringy. Avoid any large beans that have curled, have patches of brown or mould, or look dried at the ends. Place in a plastic bag and store in the refrigerator for up to 3 days.

HEALTHY BENEFITS

Runner beans have a high water content and are a good source of carotene. They contain phytic acid and lectins. They should not be eaten raw.

PREPARATION TECHNIQUES

The majority of runner beans have to be strung before cooking. This means removing a tough, stringy strip from both sides of the beans. Some homes will have a little gadget to pass the beans through to remove the strings and cut the beans into thin strips. These can be hard to find in the shops.

1 Start by selecting the number of beans you require.

2 Trim off the tops and tails.

3 Using a small, sharp knife, remove the stringy part that runs down the side of each bean. You should wash them at this stage.

4 Cut them at an angle into thin strips.

To cook them, plunge the prepared beans into lightly salted, boiling water and bring back to the boil. Cook for about 3–5 minutes, until the beans are bright green and slightly crisp. Drain and serve.

lime & ginger pork chop with stir-fried runner beans   SERVES 1

This dish could also be made with lean pork loin steaks or skinless chicken breast.

lean pork chop	1 (approx 150g/5oz)
sunflower oil	2 tsp
chicken/vegetable stock	4 tbs
dark soy sauce	1 tsp
honey	¼ tsp
finely chopped fresh ginger	½
lime, thinly sliced	½
thick egg noodles	25g/⅓ cup

stir-fried runner beans

garlic	1 small clove
spring onions/scallions or green onions	2
runner beans/string beans	75g/1 cup
button mushrooms	50g/½ cup
chilli powder	pinch
dark soy sauce	1 tsp
sesame seeds (optional)	½ tsp

equipment

Medium frying pan	Small baking tray or
Medium saucepan	roasting pan

- Preheat the oven to 200°C/400°F/Gas Mark 6.
- Trim the pork chop of any excess fat. Heat a medium-sized non-stick frying pan, add 1 tsp of the oil and add the chop and brown on both sides. Transfer to a foil-lined baking tray or small roasting pan.
- Pour the stock into the frying pan, and allow to bubble up then stir in the dark soy sauce, honey and ginger. Pour over the chop, arrange the lime slices on top and bake for 20 minutes, basting occasionally with the glaze.
- Meanwhile, put the noodles into a pan with boiling water, cook for 3 minutes, then remove from the heat and stand.
- Peel and finely chop the garlic, trim the onions and chop.
- Prepare the beans as described on page 103.
- Wash the frying pan, reheat and add the rest of the oil. Cook the garlic and onions for 1 minute, add the prepared beans and mushrooms and stir fry together for 3 minutes. Add the chilli powder and soy sauce and a tablespoon of water, and cook for 2 minutes.
- Drain the noodles and add to the vegetables, scatter over the sesame seeds (if using). Spoon onto a plate, place the pork chop alongside and spoon over any juices left in the foil.

FROM START TO FINISH: 30 MINUTES

luxury masala omelette   SERVES 1

One of the most perfect dishes to make for yourself, there are endless way to make an omelette, perfect for a quick and easy meal.

sunflower oil	1 tsp
small onion, sliced	1
small green pepper, chopped	½
Tikka paste	1 tsp
tomato, halved	1
fresh coriander, shredded	Few sprigs
garam masala	Pinch
butter	Small knob
eggs, beaten	2 large
salt and freshly ground pepper	

equipment

Small non-stick frying pan   Rubber spatula

- Heat the oil in a small frying pan, add the onion and pepper and fry for 2 minutes until beginning to brown. Add the tikka paste and tomato and stir over a medium heat for 2 minutes. Stir in the coriander and garam masala, then tip into a bowl and cover to keep warm.

- Wash the pan, dry and put back on the heat. Add the butter and, when foaming, pour in the eggs and seasonings and cook on medium-high. Using the spatula, pull the set egg from the edges into the middle, allowing the runny egg to fill in the gaps. Cook until set and the underside is golden-brown.

- Spoon the filling into the middle, fold over the omelette then lift onto a hot plate and eat at once.

FROM START TO FINISH: 15 MINUTES

tomato & rocket spaghetti   **SERVES 1**

Pasta is such a great dish for mid-week quick meals, and the sauce takes minutes to prepare. There is no need to buy a jar of ready made.

spaghetti	50g/2 oz
olive oil	1 tsp
red pepper, cut into small strips	½
garlic, finely chopped	1 clove
chopped tomatoes	225g/8-oz can
pesto sauce	1 tsp
low-fat crème fraiche	2 tbs
salt and freshly ground black pepper	
rocket	25g/⅓ cup
freshly grated or shaved Parmesan cheese (optional)	1 tbs

equipment

Medium saucepan   Colander/strainer
Small saucepan

- Bring a medium pan of lightly salted water to the boil, hold the spaghetti in the water and as it softens, allow it to fall into the water, give it a stir then cook for 12–15 minutes, until just tender. To test, lift a strand out of the pan and bite the end, it should be the same texture all the way through and not hard in the middle.

- While the pasta is cooking, heat a small pan with the oil and cook the peppers for 2–3 minutes until beginning to soften, add the garlic and cook 1 minute. Stir in the tomatoes and their juice and simmer for 5 minutes until the mixture becomes pulpy. Stir in the pesto sauce and crème fraiche and heat through.

- Drain the pasta in a colander or sieve, return to the pan. Add the sauce with the rocket and toss together, serve with grated Parmesan cheese if preferred.

FROM START TO FINISH: 15 MINUTES

sicilian-style tuna & herbed vegetables   SERVES 1

Fresh tuna is readily available and perfect for cooking on a griddle or the barbecue. The trick is not to overcook it, as it can dry out.

The secret of successful griddling is to get the pan very hot so the food seals on contact, then the heat can be reduced so the food cooks through.

Also, brush only the food with oil – if you brush the griddle, too much oil falls between the ridges and will smoke badly during cooking, fogging up the kitchen.

small new potatoes	115g/⅔ cup
courgette/zucchini	1 medium
red pepper	½
fresh tuna steak	150g/¾ cup
salt and freshly ground	
black pepper	
olive oil	4 tsp
lemon (grated zest)	½
lemon juice	2 tsp
garlic, finely chopped	½ clove
capers, rinsed	1 tsp
freshly chopped flat	1 tbs
leaved parsley	

equipment

Small saucepan   Griddle pan

- Put the potatoes to cook in a pan of lightly salted water, boil for 12–15 minutes until just tender. Preheat a griddle pan to hot.
- Trim the courgettes/zucchini and cut lengthways into long thin strips, cut the pepper into wide strips, lightly brush with oil. Put the tuna onto a plate and also brush with oil, season.
- Lay the strips of vegetables in the griddle pan to cook over a medium-high heat for about 5–8 minutes, turning when they have golden-brown stripes.
- There should be 2 tsp of oil remaining, put into a bowl, add the lemon zest, juice, garlic, capers and herbs.
- When all the vegetables are cooked, remove and keep warm. Place the tuna on the hot griddle pan and cook for 2–3 minutes on each side (depending on the thickness of the steak) until just cooked, but slightly pink in the middle. Drain the potatoes.
- Serve the tuna on a bed of the vegetables, spoon over the herb dressing and add the potatoes, halved if preferred.

FROM START TO FINISH: 25 MINUTES

stir-fried beef with broccoli   SERVES 4

basmati rice	50g/¼ cup
broccoli	150g/1½ cups
oyster mushrooms	50g/½ cup
cornflour	½ tsp
soy sauce	2 tsp
rice vinegar or	1 tsp each
dry sherry and sesame oil	
five-spice powder	Pinch
garlic	1 clove
onion or shallot	1 very small
lean rump or sirloin steak	115g/4-oz
sunflower oil	2 tsp

equipment

Large non-stick frying pan	Colander/strainer
Small saucepan	Tongs

- Put the rice to cook in a small pan with boiling salted water for 10 minutes or until tender. Drain when cooked.
- Meanwhile, cut the broccoli into equal-sized small florets, then drop into a pan of boiling water and boil for 3 minutes. Drain through a sieve. Tear the mushrooms into wide strips if they are large.
- In a small bowl mix the cornflour, with 2 tbsp water, soy sauce, vinegar, sesame oil, and five-spice powder.
- Thinly slice the garlic, thickly slice the onion and slice the steak thinly across the grain into slices 5cm/2 inches long.
- Heat the sunflower oil in a non-stick frying pan or a wok, add the oil and then the garlic, after a few seconds add the onion, beef and mushrooms and stir fry for 3 minutes until browned. You may need to turn the meat with tongs so it cooks evenly. Stir in the soy sauce mixture and bubble up, then add the broccoli and cook 1–2 minutes to heat through.
- Serve with cooked basmati rice.

FROM START TO FINISH: 15 MINUTES

Friends never fail to admire real home cooking, particularly with something tasty, but what a great host you will be when you treat your family and friends to dishes that are healthy too.

cooking to impress

cajun chicken kebabs with avocado salsa SERVES 4

These kebabs can be served with couscous (see page 127, North African Chicken and Apricot Casserole) and some halved cherry tomatoes or Summer Rice Salad (see page 60).

coriander seeds	1 tsp
salt	½ tsp
paprika	2 tsp
cayenne pepper	½ tsp
mustard powder	1 tsp
ground black pepper	½ tsp
soft light brown sugar	2 tsp
lime	1
skinless chicken breasts	4
olive oil	2 tbs
red pepper	1
green pepper	1

avocado salsa

avocado	1 medium
red onion	½ small
vine ripened tomato	1 large
garlic	1 clove
red chilli	½–1 large
coriander	small handful
salt and freshly ground black pepper	

equipment

Small frying pan	Knife
Pestle and mortar	2 small bowls
Medium bowls	Metal skewers
Grater	Barbecue or grill/broiler

- To make the 'rub', put the coriander seeds into a small frying pan and dry-fry for a few minutes until golden. Transfer to the pestle and mortar and crush. Transfer to a bowl and add the salt, spices, pepper and sugar.
- Grate the zest from the lime and mix into the rub.
- Cut the chicken into bite-sized pieces, put into a glass bowl, add the oil and toss together. Scatter in the rub and toss again. Cover and refrigerate for 1 hour.
- Cut the tops off the peppers, remove the seeds, then cut into pieces roughly the same size as the chicken.
- To prepare the salsa, halve the avocado lengthways, remove the stone then peel away the skin. Cut into small pieces and put into a bowl. Finely chop the onion, halve the tomato, remove the core then chop into small dice, peel and finely chop the garlic, and remove the seeds from the chilli and chop fine. Add all these ingredients to the avocado. Squeeze the juice from the lime, chop the coriander, then stir both into the salsa and season as needed.
- Thread the chicken onto metal skewers alternatively with the pieces of pepper.
- Place on a prepared barbecue or grill/broiler and cook for 10–15 minutes, turning the skewers until the chicken is golden brown and the peppers slightly charred at the edges.

FROM START TO FINISH: 45 MINUTES, PLUS 1 HOUR MARINATING TIME

lebanese fattoush   SERVES 4–6

Based on a Lebanese recipe, it makes good use of wholemeal pitta bread, particularly if it is a little dry. Serve as a starter or to accompany a light meal or grilled/broiled or barbecued foods.

wholemeal pitta breads	3
olive oil	1 tbs
trimmed head romaine or cos lettuce	1 small
green pepper	1
plum or large vine-ripened tomatoes	5
red onion	1
cucumber	½
radishes	10
mint or basil	small handful
flat-leaved parsley	large handful

dressing

garlic	1–2 cloves
coarse salt	1 tsp
lemon (juice)	1
extra virgin olive oil	5 tbs
freshly ground black pepper	

- Pre-heat the oven to 200°C/400°F/Gas Mark 6.
- Brush the pitta bread with the oil, place on the baking tray and place in the oven for 10 minutes until golden and crisp. Tear or chop into small pieces or strips. Put to one side.
- Shred the lettuce and put into a large shallow bowl.
- Remove the seeds from the pepper and cut into dice. Dice the tomatoes and finely chop the onion. Add to the bowl.
- The cucumber can be peeled if preferred, then cut into dice. Trim and slice the radishes. Add to the salad.
- Chop the herbs and combine with the salad ingredients. Leave to stand for 10 minutes. Scatter in the pitta bread pieces.
- For the dressing, crush the garlic with the salt, put into a small bowl and whisk in the other dressing ingredients. Pour over the salad and toss together.
- Leave to stand for an hour to allow the pitta bread to soak up some of the juices and dressing. Serve at room temperature.

FROM START TO FINISH: 25 MINUTES

equipment

Pastry brush	Small bowl
Baking tray	Whisk
Sharp knife	Citrus squeezer
Large bowl	

1

4

2

5

3

step-by-step

tomatoes

BUYING AND STORING

There is a wide variety of tomatoes available all year round, though many imported tomatoes do not have the full flavour of seasonal home-grown ones. Look for firm, deep-coloured tomatoes without any soft spots. Check the stalk end (calyx), as this is a good indication of freshness, it should be fresh and green in appearance.

When ripening tomatoes, they should be kept in a single layer for up to a week. Try not to store them in the refrigerator as this can spoil the texture of the tomato. If you do store them in the refrigerator, bring them to room temperature, before using raw, to get the best flavour.

HEALTHY BENEFITS

Tomatoes are rich in lycopene, the antioxidant phytochemical which is important in helping to prevent cancers and heart disease. Lycopene is more potent in cooked and canned tomatoes and tomato pastes, purées and juices than in raw tomatoes. They also contain the antioxidants beta-carotene and vitamin C and E

PREPARATION TECHNIQUES

For general use, remove the calyx and wash under cold running water. Dry on kitchen paper. For slicing and cutting, use a serrated knife. Place the tomato on a board, with the stalk end down, and slice the fruit downwards.

To Peel:

1 Start by selecting some tomatoes. It is probably better to use quite large tomatoes.

2 Remove the green stalk from the tomatoes.

3 Cut a cross in the top of the tomatoes at the stem end. Place in a bowl and cover with boiling water. Leave them to stand for 30 seconds. Lift them out of the hot water with a spoon and plunge them into a bowl of cold water.

4 Drain, then gently peel off the skin.

5 Depending on what you're cooking, you may then want to chop the tomatoes.

pork frikadeller SERVES 4

Meatballs are very popular with both children and adults, but taste so much better when you make your own. Not always cooked with a tomato sauce, but it adds both taste and goodness from the fresh tomatoes.

day-old wholegrain bread	2 slices
semi-skimmed milk	120ml/½ cup
onion, grated	1 small
minced pork	500g/1lb 2oz
beaten egg	½
1 tsp English mustard	
nutmeg	large pinch
salt and freshly ground	
black pepper	
rapeseed/canola oil	2 tbs
half-fat crème fraiche	2 tbs

sauce

fresh tomatoes	500g/1lb 2oz
onion	1 medium
garlic	2 cloves
olive oil	1 tbs
tomato purée/paste	1 tbs
sugar	pinch
salt and freshly ground	
black pepper	

- Put the bread in a dish and soak in the milk for 10 minutes.
- To prepare the sauce, peel the tomatoes as shown on page 119. Roughly chop the tomatoes and put into a bowl with their juices. Peel the onion and chop into small dice. Peel the garlic and crush. Heat the oil in a medium saucepan and cook the onions gently for 4–5 minutes until softened. Add the garlic and cook for 1 minute, then add the tomatoes, tomato purée and sugar, season with salt and pepper and simmer for 15 minutes.
- To prepare the meatballs, squeeze dry the bread and break it up in a bowl. Add the onion, minced pork, egg and seasonings, working the mixture together with your hands. Pinch off walnut-sized pieces and roll in your palm to make small balls.
- Heat the oil in a large frying pan, add the pork balls and fry 8–10 minutes over a medium-high heat, turning them all the time until lightly browned all over. Skim off any excess oil, pour over the tomato sauce and simmer for a further 5 minutes, turning the meatballs in the sauce. Stir in the crème fraiche and season if needed.

FROM START TO FINISH: 45 MINUTES

equipment

3 large bowls	Medium saucepan
Knife	Large non-stick frying pan
Sieve	Spatula

heavenly roast chicken & vegetable salad SERVES 4

chicken	1.5kg/3½lb
salt and ground pepper	
lemon (juice of)	1
garlic	3–4 cloves
of thyme or tarragon	a few sprigs
olive oil	1 tbs

vegetables

aubergine/eggplant, trimmed and cut into 2.5 cm/1-inch pieces	1 medium
courgettes/zucchini, cut into 1 cm/½-inch slices	2 medium
red onions, cut into wedges	2
red pepper (wide strips)	1
yellow pepper, (wide strips)	1
olive oil	2 tbs
dried Italian herbs	1 tsp
cherry tomatoes	225g/1¼ cups
Balsamic vinegar	1 tbs

equipment

Kitchen roll/paper towel	Carving board
1 medium roasting pan with grid	Metal skewer, to test chicken
	Glass bowl
1 large roasting tin	Small saucepan or bowl
Rubber spatula	

- Heat the oven to 220°C/425°F/Gas Mark 7.
- Pull off any fat from the chicken and rinse the inside with cold water. Drain and pat dry with kitchen paper. Season the cavity and insert the squeezed lemon halves, garlic and herbs to flavour. Place on a roasting pan, rub on a tablespoon of the oil, season with salt and pepper and pour half of the lemon juice over. Oven cook for 15 minutes. Reduce heat to 190°C/375°F/Gas Mark 5 and cook for 25 minutes more.
- While the chicken is cooking, put the prepared aubergine, courgettes, onions, peppers, oil, dried herbs and seasonings into a large roasting tin. Toss together using the spatula.
- Take the chicken out of the oven and turn over, breast side down, and pour over the rest of the lemon juice. Place the vegetables on the top shelf of the oven and the chicken underneath. Continue to cook for 25 minutes.
- Remove both trays from the oven. Turn the chicken over and baste with the juices in the pan, turn the vegetables and add the cherry tomatoes. Return trays to the oven.
- Cook a further 10–15 minutes to crisp up the skin on the chicken. To test that it's cooked through, pierce the thickest part of the thigh with the skewer. If the juices run clear, the chicken is ready. Transfer the chicken to a carving board and leave to stand, in a warm place, for 10 minutes.
- Turn the oven up a little and continue to cook the vegetables a further 10–15 minutes. Pour the juices from the chicken's roasting tin into a glass bowl. Allow to settle, then skim off all the fat and discard. The rest can be reheated in a small pan or microwave if wished.
- Take out the vegetables, sprinkle over the balsamic vinegar and transfer to a warm serving dish. Carve the chicken into thick slices and pour over the lemony garlic-flavoured juices. Serve with the vegetables.

FROM START TO FINISH: 1 HOUR 20 MINUTES

lime & chilli prawns with noodles SERVES 4

Using ready-cooked noodles will save you some time with this dish. If you prefer to use other pasta, boil for 10 minutes (or as directed on the packaging) before adding to the prawns-and-lime mixture.

lime	1
cornflour	1 tsp
brown sugar	1 tsp
soy sauce	2 tbs
Chinese chilli sauce	2 tbs
garlic	2 cloves
fresh ginger	5 cm/2-inch piece
red pepper	1
sugar snaps	175g/1½ cups
spring onions/scallions or green onions	1 bunch
pak choi	200g/7-oz packet
rapeseed/canola oil	2 tbs
frozen raw king prawns, thawed	2 × 200g/7-oz bags
vegetable stock	150ml/⅔ cup
ready cooked fine noodles	2 × 140g/5-oz packets

- Finely grate the lime rind into a bowl, then squeeze the juice. Stir in the cornflour, sugar, soy sauce and chilli sauce.
- Peel and finely chop the garlic and ginger. Remove the seeds from the pepper and cut into thin slices.
- Trim the onions and chop, and cut the pak choi into long, wide strips.
- Heat a large frying pan or wok, add 1 tablespoon of the oil and then, when hot, add the garlic and ginger. Cook for 30 seconds, add the prawns and stir fry for about 3 minutes until the prawns are pink. Tip into a bowl. Wipe out the pan with kitchen paper, as any bits of garlic and ginger left in the pan may burn.
- Reheat the pan and add the rest of the oil. When hot, add the pepper and sugar snaps. Stir fry for 2 minutes, then add onions and pak choi and cook for 2 minutes.
- Return the prawns to the pan with the lime mixture, stock and noodles and heat through, tossing together, until the sauce is thickened and the noodles are separated and hot.

FROM START TO FINISH: 25 MINUTES

equipment

Grater	Large frying pan or wok
Small bowl	Large bowl
Citrus squeezer	Kitchen roll/paper towel
Knife	

tuscan chicken **SERVES 4**

Although sometimes made with cannellini beans, the slate green Puy lentils give this an authentic Italian flavour while being quick and easy to cook, as they do not require soaking.

olive oil	2 tbs
skinless chicken breasts	4
onion, chopped	1 medium
garlic, chopped fine	2 cloves
red pepper, de-seeded and cut into 1 cm/½-inch dice	1
white wine	150ml/⅔ cup
chicken stock	350ml/1½ cups
puy lentils	115g/¾ cup
chopped tomatoes	225g/8-oz can
rosemary spikes, roughly chopped	1 tbs
salt and freshly ground black pepper	

- Heat a sauté pan (with lid), add half the oil and the chicken breasts and cook on each side 2–3 minutes until beginning to colour. Remove from the pan. Add the remaining oil and onion and cook over a medium heat 4–5 minutes until soft and golden. Stir in the garlic and pepper and cook for 1 minute.

- Pour in the wine and bring to the boil, boil 1 minute then pour in the chicken stock. Put the lentils in a sieve and rinse under cold water, then stir them into the mixture along with the chopped tomatoes.

- Bring the sauce to simmer, add the rosemary and return the chicken to the pan. Cover the pan and cook gently for 25 minutes or until the chicken and lentils are tender. Season with salt and pepper if needed, and serve with a crisp green salad.

FROM START TO FINISH: 45 MINUTES

equipment

Sharp knife Sieve
Sauté pan with lid

north african chicken & apricot casserole SERVES 4

Harissa paste can be used in casseroles or marinades or rubbed onto chicken breast fillets or lamb chops before grilling/broiling; here it adds a kick to the couscous. Cold couscous, harissa, chopped cucumber, tomatoes and herbs make a great salad. Adding chickpeas towards the end of this dish will bulk it up.

saffron threads	large pinch
chicken stock	450ml/2 cups
olive oil	1 tbs
onion, sliced fine	1 medium
garlic, finely chopped	2 cloves
each ground cinnamon and ginger	½ tsp
ground cumin	1 tsp
coriander, chopped	small handful
skinless chicken breasts	4
dried apricots, halved	175g/¾ cup
couscous	175g/1 cup
vegetable stock	240ml/1 cup
harissa paste	1–2 tsp
olive oil (lemon-flavoured if available)	2 tbs

- Put the saffron threads into a measuring jug and pour over 150ml/⅔ cup of the hot stock. Heat up a deep sauté pan, add the oil and then the onions and cook for 3–4 minutes until they soften and begin to colour. Add the garlic and spices and cook for 1 minute. Add the saffron liquid.
- Place the chicken breasts in the pan, pour in the rest of the stock, scatter over the apricots. Bring to simmer, then cover the pan and simmer for 40 minutes, stirring twice during cooking.
- Meanwhile, put the couscous in a bowl and pour over the vegetable stock, stir in the harissa paste. Cover and leave for 10 minutes until all the stock is absorbed. Fluff up the couscous with a fork, breaking up any clumps, then add the oil and stir through. Cover the bowl with a plate and reheat for 1 minute in the microwave just before serving.
- When the chicken is tender, remove from the pan, then boil the liquid for 3–4 minutes until it is reduced by about half and thickens a little. Return the chicken to the pan to reheat, then serve with the couscous.

FROM START TO FINISH: 55 MINUTES

equipment

Measuring jug   Sauté pan (with lid)
Sharp knife   Medium bowl

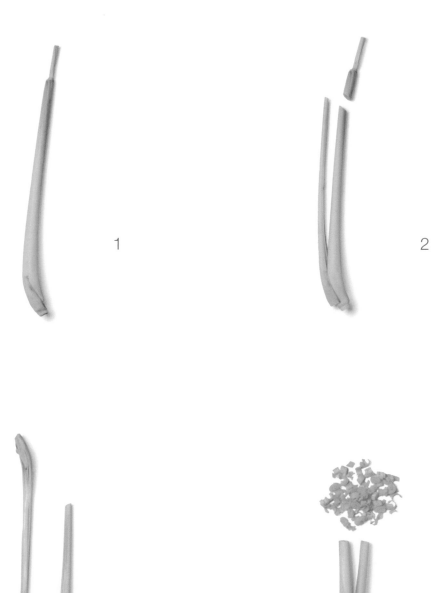

1

2

3

4

step-by-step

lemon grass

BUYING AND STORING

The name lemon grass includes several species of grass that all possess the flavour of lemon, due to the presence of citric oils. It is a useful flavouring for fish and chicken dishes, salads and soups, particularly those with an Asian theme.

When choosing lemon grass, look for plump, fresh-looking bulbs with a creamy yellow colour. Avoid any that looks very dry and withered and brown around the edges and top of the stalk. It will keep for up to 2 weeks if stored in the refrigerator.

HEALTHY BENEFITS

Lemon grass is valued for its antiseptic qualities. It can be drunk to relieve the symptoms of colds and flu: chop a stalk or two, put it into a mug with some boiled water, and then allow to infuse.

PREPARATION TECHNIQUES

1 Start by selecting a decent-sized stalk.

2 Trim the top from the lemon grass.

3 Remove the tough outer layer, then cut in half lengthways.

4 Finely chop the lemon grass.

spicy thai fishcakes   SERVES 6 AS A STARTER, 4 AS A MAIN COURSE

These can be served as a starter or as a main course with the Thai salad (see page 62).

basmati rice	50g/¼ cup
red chilli	1 large
lemon grass	1 bulb
lime (juice of)	1 large
freshly chopped coriander	1 tbs
white fish fillets such as cod, haddock	450g/1lb
nam pla (Thai fish sauce) or light soy sauce	1 tbs
red Thai curry paste	1 tbs
chopped fresh coriander	1 tbsp
salt	
sunflower oil	1 tbs

dipping sauce

fresh ginger	1 tsp
sugar	2 tsp
light soy sauce	3 tbs

equipment

Small saucepan	Baking tray
Small bowl	Large non-stick frying pan
Food processor	Spatula

- Put the rice into a small pan of boiling salted water and cook for 10–12 minutes until tender.
- While it is cooking, remove the seeds from the chilli and chop finely. Put half into a bowl for the dipping sauce and the rest in the food processor.
- Finely chop the lemon grass (see page 129) then add to the processor with 1 tbs of the lime juice and the coriander.
- Remove any skin from the fish, roughly chop into chunks and put into the food processor with the *nam pla*, curry paste and coriander. Season with a little salt then blend until finely chopped.
- Using wet hands, divide the mixture into 12 small cakes. These can be placed on a small tray, covered and refrigerated for now.
- For the sauce, finely chop the ginger and mix with the reserved chopped chilli along with the sugar, soy sauce and remaining lime juice.
- Heat a large non-stick frying pan, add the oil and the fish cakes. Cook for 4–5 minutes over a medium heat, turning until each side is golden and firm. Remove from the pan and serve with the dipping sauce, which can be spooned over the fishcakes.

FROM START TO FINISH: 40 MINUTES

mediterranean fish stew   SERVES 4

This is almost a complete meal, needing just a green salad or a bowl of steamed vegetables as an accompaniment. Serve with a spoon as well as a fork so that the juices can be eaten as soup.

Although this recipe uses a white fish you can also use salmon, tuna, monkfish or any other firm fish along with the shellfish.

new potatoes	225g/1½ cups
onion	1 small
red pepper	1
fennel	1 head
garlic	4 cloves
paprika	1 tsp
plum tomatoes	450g/1lb
olive oil	1 tbs
dry white wine	240ml/1 cup
cod fillet	250g/9oz
frozen mixed seafood, thawed	400g/14-oz bag
salt and freshly ground black pepper	
parsley, chopped	

equipment

Sharp knife	Sieve
Medium saucepan	Large saucepan or sauté pan

- Cut the potatoes in half, put into a pan with slightly salted water, bring to the boil and cook for 10 minutes.
- While the potatoes are cooking, finely chop the onion, remove the seeds from the pepper and cut into slices. Trim the stalk from the fennel then cut into 1 cm/½-inch chunks. Peel and thinly slice the garlic. Skin the tomatoes (see page 119) and roughly chop.
- Drain the potatoes.
- Heat a large saucepan or deep sauté pan, add the oil and then the onion, pepper and fennel and cook for 5 minutes over a low heat. Add the garlic and paprika and cook for a further minute.
- Add the tomatoes and wine into the pan; bring to simmer. Add the potatoes and cook for 10 minutes.
- Meanwhile cut the fish into large chunks, then add to the pan with the seafood and cook for 5–8 minutes until the fish flakes and the seafood have heated through.
- Season if needed, and scatter over some parsley.

FROM START TO FINISH: 45 MINUTES

indonesian nasi goreng   SERVES 4

This traditional Indonesian dish can be served with a tomato salad. It's also a great way to use up leftovers, particularly cooked rice. Feel free to customize this with extra vegetables.

The secret of this dish is to have the rice well drained – if it is too wet the dish will be stodgy. Add the amount of fresh chilli and chilli sauce to suit your palate.

basmati rice	225g/1¼ cups
onion	1 medium
fresh root ginger	1cm/½-inch piece
garlic	2 cloves
fresh green chillies	1 or 2 small
carrots	2
chicken breast	300g/10oz
spring onions/scallions or green onions, to garnish	4
eggs	2
rapeseed/canola oil	2 tbs
chilli sauce	½–1 tsp
paprika	1 tsp
peeled prawns, thawed if frozen	175g/1½ cups
light soy sauce	2 tbs
salt and freshly ground black pepper	to taste

equipment

Sieve	Small bowl
Large saucepan	Small frying pan
Knife	Large deep frying pan

- Put the rice in a sieve, rinse under cold water then add to a pan of boiling, salted water and cook for 12 minutes.
- Meanwhile, chop the onion, peel and finely chop the ginger and garlic. Remove the seeds from the chillies and finely chop (see page 29). Chop the carrot into very small dice and cut the chicken into small pieces. Thinly slice the onions and put to one side.
- Beat the eggs together and heat a small frying pan, adding a teaspoon of the oil. Pour the eggs in and allow them to run evenly over the base. Cook until the mixture sets into a pancake-style omelette, then turn onto a plate. Roll up tightly and set to one side, seam-side down.
- Drain the rice and rinse well with cold water, then drain again.
- Heat a large non-stick deep frying pan or sauté pan, add the rest of the oil and then the onion, ginger, garlic, chillies and carrot. Fry for 2 minutes. Add the chicken and stir fry for 3–4 minutes until it changes colour all over.
- Stir in the chilli sauce, paprika and rice, giving the mixture a good stir so the rice is covered in the spices. Add the prawns and cook for 5–6 minutes, tossing the mixture together until piping hot.
- Finally add the soy sauce and seasonings if needed.
- Cut the omelette into thin strips, turn the nasi goreng mixture into a serving dish and garnish with the omelette strips and chopped onions.

FROM START TO FINISH: 35 MINUTES

turkish stuffed aubergine   SERVES 4

This is a superb way to cook aubergine and perfect for a vegetarian meal. They can be eaten hot or cold.

bulgur wheat	40g/⅓ cup
aubergines/eggplants	2 large
salt	1 tbs
Spanish onion	1
garlic	3 cloves
olive oil	3 tbs
plum tomatoes, roughly chopped	400g/14-oz can
tomato purée/paste	1 tbs
sugar	pinch
dried oregano	1 tsp
ground cinnamon	½ tsp
coriander, chopped	large handful
pinenuts	25g/¼ cup
salt and freshly ground black pepper	

equipment

Medium bowl	Large non-stick frying pan
Serrated knife	Roasting pan
Colander/strainer	Sieve
Kitchen roll/paper towel	

- Put the bulgur wheat into a bowl, cover with hot water and leave to soak. Preheat the oven to 180°C/350°F/Gas Mark 4.
- Trim the stalks from the aubergines, cut in half lengthwise and then scoop out the flesh, leaving a 5-mm/¼-inch border, this may be made easier using a serrated grapefruit knife. Sprinkle the shells with the salt and place in a colander to drain for 15 minutes. Chop the flesh into small dice.
- Peel and chop the onion. Peel and finely chop the garlic. Heat 2 tbs of the oil in a large frying pan, add the onion and cook over a medium heat for 10 minutes until soft. Add the chopped aubergine and garlic and cook until the aubergine begins to soften, about 5 minutes.
- While the filling is cooking, rinse the aubergine shells in cold water and dry on kitchen paper. Brush the insides with the remaining oil, place side by side in the roasting pan and place in the oven to cook for 20 minutes.
- Stir into the filling mixture the tomatoes, purée, sugar, oregano and cinnamon and cook gently for 10 minutes, stirring all the time. Drain any excess liquid from the bulgur wheat and add to the mixture with the coriander and pinenuts, then season.
- Spoon the filling into the shells and return to the oven to bake for 30 minutes. Serve with a green salad.

FROM START TO FINISH: 1 HOUR 10 MINUTES

Eating raw fresh fruit is perfect as part of a healthy diet, but we all like a dessert occasionally. These ideas will inspire you to prepare fruit in a simple and imaginative way to create the perfect ending for a special meal.

sweet endings

rhubarb clafouti   SERVES 4–6

This dessert can also be made with other fruits. Try using fresh cherries in season (make sure to remove the stones first).

butter, melted	25g/⅛ cup
rhubarb	450g/1lb
orange	1
fruit sugar	50g/¼ cup

batter

wholemeal plain/ all-purpose flour	75g/⅔ cup
medium eggs	2
semi-skimmed milk	300ml/1⅓ cups
fruit sugar	50g/¼ cup
vanilla extract	1 tsp
icing sugar if desired	

- Pre-heat the oven to 200°C/400°F/Gas Mark 6. Brush the ovenproof dish with a little of the melted butter.
- Trim the ends off the rhubarb and cut into 2.5 cm/1-inch lengths. Put into the ovenproof dish.
- Cut very thin strips of orange rind with the zester and scatter them over the rhubarb. Sprinkle on the fruit sugar.
- For the batter, put all the ingredients with the remaining melted butter into a bowl and whisk together until smooth, or blend together in a blender.
- Pour the batter over the fruit and bake for 35 minutes or until golden and the rhubarb is tender. Dust with icing sugar if wished. Serve warm.

FROM START TO FINISH: 45 MINUTES

equipment

Shallow ovenproof dish	Citrus zester
Sharp knife	Whisk or blender

1

2

3

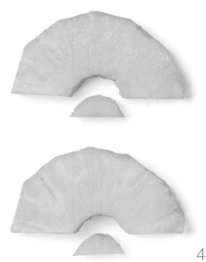

4

step-by-step preparation

pineapple

BUYING AND STORING

Choose a pineapple that is heavy for its size. If you pick it up and smell it, it should have a distinctive aroma. The skin should be firm and look fresh. It may be a golden brown colour, but some varieties have a green tinge. To check for freshness, look at the leaves – they should be crisp and firm, not brown. Avoid any pineapples that are withered around the base.

Pineapples should be ripened at room temperature then stored in the refrigerator for up to 5 days. To test if a pineapple is ripe, tug on a leaf – it should pull away from the fruit easily.

HEALTHY BENEFITS

Pineapples provide sugars, mostly as sucrose, and are a good source of vitamin C. They also contain some potassium and magnesium and the enzyme bromelain, which helps digestion by aiding the breakdown of protein. It is also this enzyme that prevents pineapple from being used with gelatine in jellies.

PREPARATION TECHNIQUES

1 Start by making sure that the pineapple is ripe.

2 Cut the top off and take a slice from the bottom.

3 Stand the pineapple upright and cut downwards to remove the peel.

4 Cut in half and then into thick slices. Carefully cut out the centre core without breaking up the slices.

Pineapple can also be cut into chunks for a fruit salad or threaded onto skewers to grill.

griddled pineapple with mango & coconut salsa

SERVES 4

Look for ready-prepared toasted coconut in the section of the supermarket where nuts and seeds are sold.

pineapple	1 medium
unsalted butter	25g/2 tbs/¼ stick
caster/superfine sugar	2 tbs

mango & coconut salsa

ripe mango	1 medium
lime	1
light muscavado sugar	1 tbs
toasted coconut flakes	25g/⅓ cup

equipment

Sharp knife	Pastry brush
Small bowl	Griddle pan
Grater	Fish slice or spatula
Citrus squeezer	

- To make the salsa, cut the skin off the mango and then cut the cheeks of flesh from the stone and cut off any flesh from the side of the stone. Cut all of this into small pieces and put into a bowl. Finely grate the rind from the lime and squeeze out the juice, stirring it into the mango with the sugar. Chop the coconut flakes into smaller pieces, then stir into the salsa.
- Prepare the pineapple as explained on page 143.
- Melt the butter and lightly brush the pineapple on each side and dust with the sugar.
- Heat a griddle pan and put the pineapple on to cook for 2 minutes on each side, using a fish slice or spatula to turn the slices.
- Serve hot with the mango salsa.

FROM START TO FINISH: 20 MINUTES

summer berry pancakes **SERVES 4**

Choose any seasonal fruit that is available, but the best ones are those that can produce a coloured juice like the cherries.

medium dry white wine	120ml/4fl oz/½ cup
water	4 tbs
fruit sugar	25g/⅛ cup
fresh cherries	150g/1 cup
arrowroot	1 tsp
water	1 tbs
rosewater (optional)	2 tsp
raspberries	150g/1 cup
fresh strawberries	115g/¾ cup

pancakes

plain/all-purpose white flour	75g/⅔ cup
oat bran	40g/⅓ cup
egg	1 large
semi-skimmed milk	300ml/1⅓ cup
butter, melted	25g/2tbs/¼ stick

equipment

Medium saucepan	18cm/7-inch non-stick
Cherry stoner	frying pan
Mixing bowl	Pastry brush
Wooden spoon	Spatula
Food processor or blender	Foil wrap
(optional)	

- Put the wine, water and sugar into a saucepan and bring to the boil, reduce to simmer 2–3 minutes. Stone the cherries, halve then add to the syrup and poach for 2 minutes.
- Blend the arrowroot and water and stir into the cherry mixture. Bring to the boil and stir until the syrup thickens. Remove from the heat and stir in the rosewater if using. Fold in the raspberries. Halve or quarter the strawberries, depending on their size, and add to the pan.
- To make the pancakes, put the flour and oat bran into a bowl, beat in the egg and a little milk with a wooden spoon. Gradually beat in the remaining milk until a smooth batter forms. Alternatively put all the ingredients in a food processor or blender and whiz to make the batter.
- Heat a small non-stick frying pan, brush with melted butter, then pour in enough batter to coat the base of the pan thinly. Cook over a medium-high heat until golden brown, turn over and cook the other side. Turn the pancake out onto a plate, cover with foil to keep warm. Repeat the process until all the batter is used.
- Serve with the warm berry sauce.

FROM START TO FINISH: 40 MINUTES

apple & blackberry crisp

SERVES 4

Bramley apples	2–3 medium (approx 700g/1½lb)
lemon (juice of)	1
ground cinnamon	½ tsp
fruit sugar	2 tbs
water	5 tbs
fresh blackberries	150g/1 cup
unsalted butter	25g/2 tbs/¼ stick
fresh granary breadcrumbs	40g/¾ cup
jumbo oats	25g/¼ cup
demerara/light brown sugar	2 tsp

- Peel the apple and cut into quarters; remove the core and then cut into chunks. Put into a saucepan with the lemon juice, cinnamon, fruit sugar and water. Heat until simmering, then cover the pan, turn the heat down and cook gently for 6–8 minutes until the apple is just tender, but not mushy. Fold in the blackberries.
- In a medium saucepan, melt the butter then mix in the breadcrumbs, oats and demerara sugar. Spread onto a baking tray and place under a medium-hot grill/broiler for 3–4 minutes, turning the mixture a few times until crisp and golden.
- Spoon the fruit into four dishes, then top with the crumble mixture. Serve warm with some low-fat yogurt.

FROM START TO FINISH: 20 MINUTES

equipment

Vegetable peeler	Citrus squeezer
Sharp knife	1 medium saucepan
1 large saucepan with lid	Baking tray

poached rosé pears

SERVES 4

fruit sugar	50g/¼ cup
rosé wine	600ml/2½ cups
lemon juice	1 tbs
cinnamon	1 stick
ripe pears, peeled, cored and halved	4
shelled pistachio nuts	50g/⅓ cup

- Put the sugar, wine, lemon juice and cinnamon stick into a large pan and bring to the boil, stirring until the sugar has dissolved. Add the pears to the pan and simmer gently for 10–15 minutes or until just tender. Lift the pears from the pan and place on a dish.
- While the pears are cooking put the nuts into small bowl and cover with boiling water. Leave to stand for 5 minutes. Strain and slip off the skins to reveal the lovely green colour of the nuts.
- Return the pan to a high heat and boil, uncovered, for about 10–15 minutes until the liquid has reduced by at least half to make a more syrupy consistency. Pour the sauce over the pears and leave to cool. Once cooled, turn them over in the syrup, cover and refrigerate. To serve, arrange the pears on serving plates and pour over the sauce then scatter over the nuts.

FROM START TO FINISH: 30–35 MINUTES, PLUS COOLING

equipment

Large saucepan	Slotted spoon
Vegetable peeler or sharp knife	Small bowl
	Colander/strainer
Teaspoon	

glossary

Al dente. An Italian term meaning 'firm to the tooth', used to describe the degree to which pasta and some vegetables are cooked.

Arrowroot. A thickening agent similar to cornflour, used mainly for fruit sauces, as it gives a clear, glossy appearance. It needs to be blended with a little liquid before being added to the sauce.

Baking powder. A raising agent, made from sodium bicarbonate and cream of tartar, used during baking (usually with plain flour) to make breads and cakes rise.

Basting. Spooning the juices and melted fat over food during cooking, to keep it moist and to help browning.

Beating. To mix ingredients together, which can be done with a fork, wooden spoon or electric mixer.

Bicarbonate of Soda. Sometimes used in baking to act as a raising agent.

Blanch. To boil briefly or to part-cook; always have the water at boiling point before adding ingredient.

Boning. To remove bones from meat, poultry or fish, often in preparation for stuffing.

Braising. A slow-cooking method used for cuts of meat, fish or vegetables, usually with a small amount of liquid such as stock or wine, in a pot or casserole with a tight-fitting lid. It may be cooked on the hob or in the oven.

Broiling. American term for grilling.

Casserole. A heavy dish that can be made from metal, enamel, earthenware or ceramic, with a close-fitting lid. It is also applied to the food that is cooked and served in this type of dish.

Char-grill. Food that is cooked on a metal grid over burning coals or charcoal. The term can nowadays be applied to food cooked on a gas barbecue.

Colander. A perforated metal or plastic draining basket.

Cornstarch. American name for cornflour.

Couscous. Processed semolina in tiny pellets, most often used in North African dishes. The products most readily available have been processed so that they only require a short soaking time and no cooking.

Creaming. Beating together fat and sugar until the mixture looks like whipped cream and is pale in colour.

Dice. To cut food into small cubes.

Dredge. To coat food lightly and evenly with a dry ingredient such as flour or icing sugar.

Extracting Juice. Citrus fruits can be halved and squeezed to extract the juice either using a squeezer, or pressing a fork into them and squeezing with your hand. If using a machine, chop the fruits or vegetables before processing, or if using a blender, process and strain the mixture.

Extract. A concentrated flavouring that is used in small quantities, such as vanilla or meat extract.

Garnish. An edible decoration, such as a herb or small piece of vegetable or fruit, which enhances the appearance of a dish.

Grease. Used to describe preparing baking tins so that the contents do not stick. Oil, margarine, butter or white vegetable fat can be applied thinly with a pastry brush.

Infusing. Steeping a flavouring or aromatic in a liquid by slowly bringing it to boiling point and then allowing it to cool.

Julienne. Cutting ingredients into match-stick sized pieces.

Liquidize. Reducing food to a pourable consistency with the help of a food processor or blender. Usually for soups or sauces.

Marinade. A mixture of ingredients usually containing oil, herbs, spices, lemon juice, wine or vinegar, or even yogurt. The purpose is to tenderize the food and add flavour to it.

Marinate. To soak meat, fish, vegetables and game before cooking in a flavoured mixture. If the recipe states 'marinate overnight', this means for at least 8 hours, something that can equally be done during the day. Be careful not to marinate delicate fish for too long as it can become soggy.

Pan-Fry. To cook tender pieces of meat in a small amount of fat or oil in a shallow pan over a high heat.

Poaching. To cook food gently in liquid at just below simmering point.

Pulses. The generic name given to dried beans, peas and lentils.

Purée. Food that had been liquidized, pounded or sieved to a smooth pulp.

Reducing. Fast-boiling a liquid in an uncovered pan to concentrate its flavour and, in some cases, thicken its consistency.

Roasting. Cooking meat by dry heat in an oven, or turning food over a flame.

Rubbing in. Mixing flour and fat together lightly with the fingertips until the mixture resembles fine breadcrumbs.

Sautéeing. Cooking small pieces of food in a small quantity of fat in a frying pan so the food browns quickly.

Seasoning. Using small quantities of salt and pepper and sometimes spices or sugar to enhance the flavour of food.

Skinning. Removing the skin from meat, fish, poultry, vegetables or fruit.

Stewing. Long, slow cooking of food immersed in water in a pot with a close-fitting lid, either on the hob or in the oven.

Stir-frying. Cooking food quickly by frying in a wok over a high heat and moving the food around all the time.

index